SPORTS FOR CHILDREN:
A Guide for Adults

ABOUT THE AUTHOR

James H. Humphrey, Professor Emeritus at the University of Maryland, has published over 60 books and 200 articles and research reports. For over four decades he has been considered an international authority on the subject of physical activity as it is concerned with total child development—physical, social, emotional, and intellectual. He has written this book from his own perspective as a sports participant from childhood through college, a parent, a teacher, a coach at all educational levels, and a university researcher.

SPORTS FOR CHILDREN:
A Guide for Adults

By

JAMES H. HUMPHREY, ED.D.

Professor Emeritus
University of Maryland

With a Foreword by

Fred C. Engh

President
Chief Executive Officer
National Youth Sports Coaches Association

CHARLES C THOMAS • PUBLISHER
Springfield • Illinois • U.S.A.

Published and Distributed Throughout the World by

CHARLES C THOMAS • PUBLISHER
2600 South First Street
Springfield, Illinois 62794-9265

© *1993 by* CHARLES C THOMAS • PUBLISHER

ISBN 0-398-05890-3

Library of Congress Catalog Card Number: 93-28285

Printed in the United States of America
SC-R-3

Library of Congress Cataloging-in-Publication Data

Humphrey, James Henry, 1911–
    Sports for children : a guide for adults / James H. Humphrey ;
with a foreword by Fred C. Engh.
        p.   cm.
    Includes bibliographical references and index.
    ISBN 0-398-05890-3
    1. Sports for children.   I. Title.
GV709.2.H85   1993
796'.01922 – dc20   93-28285
                                                                    CIP

FOREWORD

When Dr. Humphrey asked me to write the Foreword for SPORTS FOR CHILDREN: A Guide for Adults, I was both proud and somewhat hesitant. Proud, because it is an honor to be asked by your former professor to write a foreword for his book. Hesitant, because if he ever remembered how unfocused I was as a student, he may have reconsidered.

My degree in physical education from the University of Maryland provided me the opportunity for a lifetime of experience in the world of youth sports, i.e., several years spent as a physical educator, coach, and athletic director, an administrator for youth sports, national director of youth sports for the Athletic Institute, founder of the National Youth Sports Coaches Association and most of all seeing my seven children participate in youth sports. The experience has given me somewhat of a license as an expert in the field of youth sports. At least that is what Dr. Humphrey said.

Locked in a plane on my way to a speaking engagement in Hawaii, I had the chance to review Dr. Humphrey's manuscript. Believe me when I say that his book is the best I have read on children in sports, and I have read a lot.

Most academic endeavors are just that, *academic,* which means the practitioner gets through the first few chapters and gives up in frustration trying to figure out all the big words and reference material derived from researchers. Dr. Humphrey's book, however, discusses youth sports from a fair, understandable, systematic way. Perhaps what I like most about the book is that once you are finished reading you can clearly see that, if conducted properly, organized sports for children *can* play a very positive role in the physical, social, emotional, and intellectual development of the child.

As a professional working in the area of youth sports, I would like to add a few thoughts that you will not find in Dr. Humphrey's book. The subject is *ugliness* in youth sports. I know that sounds kind of harsh, but if I began telling you the number of horror stories I have witnessed and that have been told to me over the years, you, too, would agree that ugliness does exist, all too often, in youth sports. It exists because of the vicarious parents who will stop at nothing to push their child unmercifully to be a star athlete; or the father next door who, with good intentions, volunteers to coach only to emerge as a tyrant who cheats, bends the rules, and even risks the safety of children in order to fulfill his ambitions to be the league champion. It exists because thousands of leagues operated by parents (1) have no official standards to allow equal play opportunity for children, (2) have no requirements that make it mandatory that coaches are trained and monitored for their behavior, (3) have no guidelines to prevent injuries and first aid procedures should injuries occur, (4) have no policy that states that adult volunteers are drug, alcohol, and tobacco free at youth sports activities.

I contend that if recreation professionals, school administrators and parents who administer youth league sports look past the scoreboard and grasp the value of Dr. Humphrey' excellent work in SPORTS FOR CHILDREN: A Guide for Adults, they will place more importance on Plato's message from two thousand years ago, — "a child is at its learning best while at play."

Fred C. Engh
President and Chief Executive Officer
National Youth Sports Coaches Association

PREFACE

I have been involved in children's sports as a participant, observer, parent, teacher, or coach for over 70 years. At the outset I want to make it luminously clear by stating forcefully and unequivocally that it is *not* the purpose of this book to extol *or* criticize the area of children's sports. On the contrary, I want to present the facts—pro and con—as I understand them with the reader coming to his or her own conclusions.

Almost any book is the result of an author's exchange with other people. This volume is no exception. That is, along with my own personal experience in this area, I have consulted with both proponents and critics of children's sports, which included parents, professional athletes, children's coaches, school personnel, and children themselves. I have tried to merge all of this information into what I hope will be a sensible guide for those adults—coaches, parents, and others—who are involved, or plan to become involved in children's sports in a way that will always be in the best interest of the child.

In the introductory chapter a general overview of sports for children is presented, emphasizing such issues as historical background, competition, injuries, and supervision. Chapter 2 is concerned with the function of sports in child development, along with the objectives of such sports. The next four chapters go into some detail with regard to how sports can contribute to each of the components of child development—physical, social, emotional, and intellectual. Chapter 7 takes into account those movement skills that are basic to successful participation of children in sports. The following chapter gives consideration to knowledge that adults should have if they propose to teach children about sports. Chapters 9, 10, and 11 are devoted to discussions of what my studies show are the most popular team sports among children; namely, football, soccer, baseball, softball, basketball, and volleyball. Included in these chapters are explanations of various sports skills that need to be accomplished for success in these sports. A distinguishing feature of these chapters are the many games that can be used to practice the various sports skills. The final chapter is concerned with discussions of certain individual sports. These are those that were most popular among children in my studies— swimming, track and field, and gymnastics—and golf which has recently had a widespread gain in popularity with children.

A book is seldom the product of the author alone. It is almost always true that many individuals participate, at least indirectly, in some way before a book is finally "put to bed." Such is the case with this volume. In this regard I would like to express my thanks to the many children who answered the detailed questions on my own *Humphrey Sports Inventory for Children;* and to the following individuals who assisted me in the collection of these data: Mary Jo Baringhaus, Sue Krekeler, Joy Rose, Anne Van Amerongen, Kitty Yost, and Warren Zabell. Finally, I owe a debt of gratitude to certain individuals who provided me with information that was most important to the content of the book. They are: Fred C. Engh, President and Chief Executive Officer, National Youth Sports Coaches Association; Dawne Larkin, The University of Western Australia; Dennis M. Sullivan, Director of Communications, Little League Baseball, Inc.; and Joseph L. Warren, Executive Director, Prince George's County, Maryland Boys and Girls Clubs.

JAMES H. HUMPHREY

IT SHOULD BE NOTED THAT CHILDREN
AT PLAY ARE NOT PLAYING ABOUT;
THEIR GAMES SHOULD BE SEEN AS
THEIR MOST SERIOUS-MINDED BUSINESS.
Montaigne 1533–1592

CONTENTS

		Page
Foreword		v
Preface		vii

Chapter

1. AN OVERVIEW OF SPORTS FOR CHILDREN............ 3
   - Historical Background................................4
   - Competition as a Factor in Children's Sports............... 7
   - Injuries as a Factor in Children's Sports.................. 10
   - Supervision of Children's Sports...................... 12
2. CHILD DEVELOPMENT AND SPORTS................. 19
   - The Meaning of Development..........................20
   - The Physical Aspect of Personality....................... 23
   - The Social Aspect of Personality.......................... 24
   - The Emotional Aspect of Personality...................... 25
   - The Intellectual Aspect of Personality.................... 26
   - Physical Objectives of Children's Sports................... 27
   - Social Objectives of Children's Sports..................... 30
   - Emotional Objectives of Children's Sports................. 31
   - Intellectual Objectives of Children's Sports................ 34
3. PHYSICAL DEVELOPMENT OF CHILDREN THROUGH SPORTS...................... 35
   - Physical Needs of Children............................ 35
   - Guidelines for Physical Development Through Children's Sports........................ 39
   - Evaluating Contributions of Sports to Physical Development........................ 42
   - Physical Activity Yield................................ 45

4. SOCIAL DEVELOPMENT OF
    CHILDREN THROUGH SPORTS...................... 49
    Social Needs of Children................................ 51
    Guidelines for Social Development Through Sports......... 54
    Some Possibilities for
    Social Development Through Sports.................... 57
    Implications of Research in
    Social Behavior of Children......................... 58
    Evaluating Contributions of
    Sports to Social Development........................ 61

5. EMOTIONAL DEVELOPMENT OF
    CHILDREN THROUGH SPORTS...................... 65
    Factors Concerning Emotional Development.............. 66
    Emotional Needs of Children........................... 69
    Guidelines for Emotional
    Development Through Sports.......................... 72
    Opportunities for Emotional
    Development Through Sports.......................... 74
    Implications of Research in
    Emotional Behavior of Children...................... 75

6. INTELLECTUAL DEVELOPMENT OF
    CHILDREN THROUGH SPORTS...................... 81
    Intellectual Needs of Children......................... 81
    Guidelines for Intellectual
    Development Through Sports.......................... 85
    Opportunities for Intellectual
    Development Through Sports.......................... 86

7. BASIC SPORTS SKILLS FOR CHILDREN.............. 99
    Factors Involved in Skill Teaching and Learning........... 100
    Locomotor Skills...................................... 100
    Axial Skills.. 106
    Auxiliary Skills...................................... 107
    Skills of Propulsion and Retrieval...................... 109
    Skills as Specific Sports Events....................... 117

8. THE COACH OR PARENT AS
    A TEACHER OF SPORTS ACTIVITIES................ 118
    Characteristics of Good Teachers....................... 120
    Teaching and Learning in Sports....................... 121
    Some Principles of Learning Applied to Sports........... 124

Phases of the Teaching-Learning Situation 128

9. FOOTBALL AND SOCCER 135

Football 126

Football Skills 138

Stance 143

Blocking and Tackling 143

Games to Practice Football Skills 143

Flag Football 145

Soccer 146

Offensive Soccer Skills 147

Defensive Soccer Skills 149

Tackling 151

Games to Practice Soccer Skills 152

10. BASEBALL AND SOFTBALL 155

Baseball 155

Baseball Skills 156

Playing the Different Positions 160

Team Play 162

Games to Practice Baseball Skills 163

Softball 164

11. BASKETBALL AND VOLLEYBALL 166

Basketball 166

Basketball Skills 166

Team Play 174

Games to Practice Basketball Skills 175

Volleyball 176

Volleying 177

Serving 179

The Set 180

The Spike 180

The Block 181

Net Recovery 181

Team Play 181

Games to Practice Volleyball Skills 182

12. INDIVIDUAL SPORTS 185

Swimming 185

Track and Field 187

Gymnastics.. 191
Golf... 193
Bibliography... 197
Index.. 201

SPORTS FOR CHILDREN:
A Guide for Adults

Chapter 1

AN OVERVIEW OF SPORTS FOR CHILDREN

At the outset it seems appropriate to provide some working definitions for certain terms used in the title of the book. As used here I will consider *sports* to be "organized interactions of children in competitive and/or cooperative team or individual enjoyable physical activities." The term *children* includes those "boys and girls through the chronological age of 12" (Ordinarily the final year of elementary school). For purposes here *adults* are the "child overseers (parents, teachers, coaches, and others) who are currently involved, or plan to become involved in some way in children's sports.

Currently, the growth of children's sports has reached almost unbelievable proportions. Using Little League Baseball as an example, at the end of the 1992 season there were 2.6 million participants on over 180,000 teams in 63 countries. In addition, more than 750,000 volunteers worldwide participated in this program.

As mentioned previously, the highest age level considered here is one reached by most children in the last year of elementary school (6th grade). Children's sports, as conceived here, are not a prominent part of most elementary school programs. There are a few remote instances where elementary schools support interscholastic or varsity sports programs, but for the most part this is quite rare. On the other hand, the major emphasis is placed on a well-balanced physical education program where all children have an equal opportunity to participate. However, some elementary schools provide sports programs in the form of *intramural* activities. This is a natural outgrowth of the physical education program with teams organized so that one classroom may play against another. This usually occurs after school and is supervised by school officials.

The great preponderance of children's sports programs take place outside of school and are not ordinarily conducted under the supervision of the school. They are usually sponsored by such organizations as recreation centers, business enterprises, and assorted boys' and girls' clubs.

Over the years such organizations as Little League Baseball, Midget Football, Pop Warner Football, Itty Bitty Basketball, Pee Wee Golf along with a vast host of others have flourished and attracted children in fantastically large numbers, which some estimates place in excess of 30 million.

It will be the function of this introductory chapter to examine some of the facets and ramifications of this burgeoning phenomenon.

HISTORICAL BACKGROUND

Contrary to some general belief, sports experience for children is not of recent origin. In fact, educators and philosophers as far back as the early Greeks felt that sports-oriented activities might be a welcome adjunct to the total education of children. For instance, over 2,300 years ago Plato suggested that all early education should be a sort of play and develop around play situations.

In the 17th century, Locke, the Englisher philosopher, felt that children should get plenty of exercise and learn to swim early in life. Rousseau, the notable French writer held much the same opinion, believing that learning should develop from the enjoyable physical activities of childhood. These men, along with numerous others, influenced to some extent the path that children's sports was to follow through the years.

There have been periods in our history when any type of sports program was abandoned purely on the basis that body pleasure of any sort must be subjugated because this activity was associated with evil doing. The early American pioneers more or less typified this kind of puritanical thinking because there was little or no emphasis on sports for the pioneer child.

Eventually, however, attitudes changed and interest in children's sports began to emerge. Instrumental in the movement was the establishment of the first public playground in Boston in 1885. This idea soon spread nationwide with children from one playground competing in various sports activities with those from other playgrounds.

It was not long before enterprising merchants saw possibilities for advertising by sponsoring various teams, thus capitalizing by organizing the traditional neighborhood games of children. It certainly made any child proud to be wearing a shirt with "Hoopengartner's Grocery" or "Morton's Drugstore" emblazoned on the back.

In more modern times a much different outlook has characterized the area of children's sports. And much of this involves the *physical fitness* of children. In fact, over a period of several years there have been varying degrees of interest in the physical fitness of children and youth. In the early 1950s the publication of the results of six physical fitness tests (named after the authors—Kraus-Webber Tests) stimulated a great deal of concern about the physical fitness of American children. These tests had been conducted with large numbers of European children and comparisons made with the results of the tests administered to a sample of children in Westchester County, New York. The fact that this geographical area at the time was considered to be one of the country's highest socioeconomic levels made the comparison all the more "appalling."

The validity and reliability of these tests, as well as the conditions under which they were administered, tended to arouse criticism among some of the skeptics of that time. Nonetheless the results did serve the purpose of alerting American educators and laymen alike to the alleged physical status of the nation's children.

As a result, then President Eisenhower appointed Shane McCarthy, a Washington D.C. lawyer, to head a committee on Fitness of American Children and Youth. Among others, this committee consisted of assorted professional boxers and a famous racehorse trainer. While the intentions of these individuals were not necessarily questioned, at the same time their knowledge and understanding of childhood fitness was of some concern. And since that time the various Chairmen of the President's Council on Physical Fitness and Sports have been appointed mainly because of their public exposure rather than their knowledge of fitness of children. A recent example of this which had obvious political overtones was the appointment of Arnold Schwarzenegger by President Bush in 1989 as the Council's Chairman. It is doubtful that a weight lifting movie actor could serve well in a capacity that should require a basic knowledge of exercise physiology, biomechanics, child development, and other aspects concerned with the fitness of children.

Another event stimulated by the results of the Kraus-Webber tests was the President's Conference on Fitness of American Youth held in Annapolis, Maryland June 18–19, 1956. This was the first peacetime fitness conference ever held under White House auspices. In his keynote opening address to the conference, the Vice-President of the United States, Richard Nixon, made the following statements which had a direct impact on childhood fitness. "Ninety-one percent of the nation's 150,000 elementary schools have no gymnasium." And further, "Ninety percent of the nation's elementary schools have less than the recommended five acres of land for essential play areas." Such pronouncements as this from our highest level of government helped to stimulate progress in elementary school physical education programs.

A short time later in September 1956 I was one of a 100 so-called "experts" who convened in Washington, DC to study the problem of childhood fitness. This conference had a great deal of impact on the improvement of existing elementary school physical education programs as well as out-of-school sports programs.

Over the years after this thrust, childhood fitness through sports has experienced various degrees of success. Interest has continued and as a result at the present time children's sports are enjoying almost unprecedented enthusiasm.

It is interesting to note that some children's sports organizations in the form of Boys & Girls Clubs were a direct result of the Great Depression in the 1930s. An exemplary case in point is the Prince George's County, Maryland Boys and Girls Club.

As unemployment grew and breadlines lengthened, the restless youth of the County began to organize themselves into close-knit neighborhood gangs. While they were not the violent criminals of today's street gangs, their petty lawlessness became an increasing concern to the community leaders and policemen of the day.

No one knows who originated the concept of imposing a socially-approved structure onto the youths' informal organization, but the idea came to fruition in 1939 under the auspices of the County Police Department. Then, known as the Prince George's County Police Boys Clubs, the troops were jointly supervised by police officials and a group of notable County citizens.

The stated purpose of the Police Boys Clubs was to organize youth into supervised play groups, operating under traditional American patterns of sportsmanship and fair play. Even then, sports were regarded as an important activity for the improvement of a young man's physical, emotional, and moral well-being, and the Boys Clubs were operated with this principle in mind.

As the Boys Clubs became a broader community concern, the name "Police" was dropped from the title. The program remained almost exclusively a male domain until well into the 1970s, when the word "Girls" was incorporated into the Club's title.

As the program has grown in numbers, it has grown in purpose as well. Where the clubs once served primarily to "keep kids off the street," they now strive to "provide training and instruction to help young people learn and develop the principles of citizenship, good sportsmanship, knowledge of law observance, wise use of leisure time, knowledge of good health habits, and physical fitness."

Today in Prince George's County there are a total of 32 neighborhood clubs whose activities are enjoyed by over 14,000 participants, making it one of the largest Boys and Girls organizations in the nation. One of the principal reasons for the popularity of the clubs is the variety of activities they make available to their members. The 32 clubs participate in such diverse sports as baseball, bowling, volleyball, track, cheerleading, soccer, wrestling, T-ball, football, softball, and basketball.

For boys and girls—parents and volunteers—Prince George's County Boys and Girls Clubs offer excitement, friendship, and just plain fun. They are certainly one of Prince George's County's greatest sources of community spirit.

COMPETITION AS A FACTOR IN CHILDREN'S SPORTS

The positive and negative aspects of sports competition for children has been debated for decades. In fact, over 40 years ago I was the chairman of a national committee on "Competition for Children." After studying the matter with some degree of thoroughness, the "experts" on our committee decided that the success or failure of such competition was dependent upon the type of supervision provided for overseeing such programs. (Supervision of children's sports will be discussed later in the chapter.)

There has always been a concern for the emotional stress that competition can have on a child. And, of course, such emotional stress can impact on a child's physical well-being.

In a study conducted with 200 5th and 6th grade children, one of the questions I asked was "What is the one thing that *worries* you most in school?" As might be expected there were a variety of responses. However, the one general characteristic that tended to emerge was the emphasis placed on competition in so many school situations. Although students did not state this specifically, the nature of their responses clearly seemed to be along these lines.

Most of the literature on competition for children has focused on sports activities; however, there are many situations that exist in some classrooms that can cause competitive stress. An example is the anti-quated "Spelling Bee" which still exists in some schools, and in fact, continues to be recognized in an annual national competition. Perhaps the first few children "spelled down" are likely to be the ones who need spelling practice the most. And, to say the least, it can be embarrassing in front of others to fail in any school task.

It is interesting to note that the terms *cooperation* and *competition* are antonymous; therefore, the reconciliation of children's competitive needs and cooperative needs is not an easy matter. In a sense we are confronted with an ambivalent condition which, if not carefully handled, could place children in a state of conflict, thus causing them to suffer distress.

This was recognized by Horney[1] over half century ago when she indicated that we must not only be assertive but aggressive, able to push others out of the way. On the other hand, we are deeply imbued with ideals which declare that it is selfish to want anything for ourselves, that we should be humble, turn the other hand, be yielding. Thus, society not only rewards one kind of behavior (cooperation) but its direct oppo-site (competition). Perhaps more often than not our cultural demands sanction these rewards without provision of clear-cut standards of value with regard to specific conditions under which these forms of behavior might well be practiced. Thus, the child is placed in somewhat of a quandary as to when to compete and when to cooperate.

More recently it has been found that competition does not necessarily lead to peak performance, and may in fact interfere with achievement. In this connection Kohn[2] reported on a survey on the effects of competi-tion in sports, business, and classroom achievement and found that 65 studies showed that cooperation promoted higher achievement than competition, 8 showed the reverse, and 36 showed no statistically signifi-cant differences. It was concluded that the trouble with competition is that it makes one person's success depend upon another's failure, and as a result when success depends on sharing resources, competition can get in the way.

---

[1]Horney, Karen, *The Neurotic Personality of Our Times,* New York, W. W. Norton & Company, Inc., 1937.

[2]Kohn, A., *No Contest: The Case Against Competition,* Boston, Houghton-Mifflin, 1986.

In studying about competitive stress Scanlan and Passer[3] described this condition as occurring when a child feels (perceives) that he or she will not be able to perform adequately to the performance demands of competition. When the child feels this way, he or she experiences considerable threat to self-esteem which results in stress. They further described competitive stress as the negative emotion or anxiety that a child experiences when he or she perceived the competition to be personally threatening. Indeed, this is a condition that should not be allowed to prevail in any environment—school or out-of-school.

Studying the problem objectively, Scanlan[4] used a sports environment to identify predictors of competitive stress. She investigated the influence and stability of individual differences and situational factors on the competitive stress experienced by 76 9- to 14-year-old wrestlers. The subjects represented 16 teams from one state and reflected a wide range of wrestling ability and experience. Stress was assessed by the children's form of the Competitive State Anxiety Inventory and was measured immediately before and after each of two consecutive tournament matches.

The children's dispositions, characteristic precompetition cognitions, perception of significant adult influences, psychological states, self-perceptions and competitive outcomes were examined as predictors of pre- and postmatch anxiety in separate multiple regression analyses for each tournament round. The most influential and stable predictors of prematch stress for both matches were competitive stress anxiety and personal performance expectancies, while win-loss and fun experienced during the match predicted postmatch stress for both rounds.

Prematch worries about failure and perceived parental pressure to participate were predictive to Round One prematch stress. Round One postmatch stress levels predicted stress after Round Two, suggesting some consistency in the children's stress responses. Sixty-one and 35 percent prematch and 41 percent and 32 percent of postmatch state anxiety variances was explained for Rounds One and Two, respectively.

In generalizing on the basis of the available evidence with regard to the subject of competition, it seems justifiable to formulate the following concepts:

---

[3]Scanlan, Tara K. and Passer, M. W., *The Psychological and Social Affects of Competition,* Los Angeles, University of California, 1977.

[4]Scanlan, Tara K., Social Psychological Aspects of Competition for Male Youth Sport Participants: Predictors of Competitive Stress, *Journal of Sport Psychology,* 6, 1984.

1. Very young children in general are not very competitive but become more so as they grow older.
2. There is a wide variety in competition among children; that is, some are violently competitive, while others are mildly competitive, and still others are not competitive at all.
3. Boys are more competitive than girls.
4. Competition should be adjusted so that there is not a preponderant number of winners over losers.
5. Competition and rivalry can sometimes produce results in effort and speed of accomplishment.

Adults involved in children's sports might well be guided by the above concepts. Whether you are a proponent or critic of competitive sports for children, it has now become evident that such competition may be "here to stay." Thus, controlling it might be our greatest concern. This might perhaps be done by concentrating our efforts in the direction of educating both adults and children regarding the positive and negative effects of competition.

INJURIES AS A FACTOR IN CHILDREN'S SPORTS

The thing that concerns parents—particularly mothers—the most about their children's participation in sports is the possibility of injury. It should be borne in mind that contrary to popular opinion, accidents resulting in injury do not "just happen." On the other hand, over 90 percent of such accidents are caused. Although injuries do occur, many of them can be avoided if proper precautions are taken. Thus, appropriate care should be taken to assure the well-being of the child participant.

Two of my former doctoral students, Robert G. Davis and Larry D. Isaacs,[5] have devised the following set of guidelines for those responsible for conducting children's sports programs.

1. Use quality constructed and proper fitting protective gear.
2. Match teams for competition on the basis of physical fitness, skill level and physical maturation (biological age)—not chronological age only.
3. Children should not be forced into sport participation. Children who don't want to be involved in a sport are at high risk for injury.

---

[5]Davis, Robert G. and Isaacs, Larry D., *Elementary Physical Education*, Winston-Salem, NC, Hunter Textbooks, Inc., 1992.

4. Young participants should be encouraged to play different sports and experience different positions within a given activity. This practice tends to reduce injuries which may be a result of overstressing a particular movement pattern.
5. Pay close attention to signs of physical fatigue. Many injuries occur late in a game or practice session when the children are tired. Unfortunately, the image conveyed by some coaches, "be tough," keeps many young athletes from telling the coach of their fatigue.

There are certain conditions traditionally associated with sports. "Tennis elbow" is a case in point. This is an inflammation of the rounded portion of the bone at the elbow joint. The name is no doubt a misnomer because the majority of cases are a result of activities other than swinging a tennis racquet.

The same could probably be said of what has become commonly known as "Little League elbow." The technical name for this condition is *osteochondritis capitulum* which like "tennis elbow" is an inflammation of a bone and its cartilage at the elbow joint. It is caused generally by a hard and prolonged act of throwing using the overarm throwing pattern. One would not have to be a "Little Leaguer" to contract this condition. Simply playing catch and throwing hard to a partner for prolonged periods could also bring this about.

One of the most feared injuries in sports, or any activity for that matter, are those to the eyes. In this regard Orlando[6] did an interesting study to determine the severity and frequency of soccer-related eye injuries. The medical charts of 13 soccer players who had sustained blunt trauma to the eye were reviewed. The patients (five girls, eight boys) ranged in age from 8 to 15 years. The most common injury was *hyphemia* (a hemorrhage in the eyeball). Others included *retinal edema* (excessive accumulation of fluid in the innermost layer of the eye), *secondary glaucoma* (increased pressure within the eyeball), *chorioretinal rupture* (an inflammatory condition in the back of the eye), and *angle recession.* Six injuries were caused by the soccer ball, three by a kick, and one by a head butt. In three cases the cause was unknown. As a result of the study, the author made the following recommendations: (1) education of coaching staff, parents, and officials; (2) protective eye wear; (3) proper conditioning; (4) strictly enforced rules; and (5) an emphasis on having fun to help reduce the number and severity of soccer related eye injuries.

---

[6]Orland, R. G., Soccer-Related Eye Injuries in Children and Adolescents, *Physician and Sportsmedicine,* November 1988.

An interesting recent concern is one generated by spectators of the 1992 Olympic Games in Barcelona. They fear that the constant physical pounding associated with gymnastics could hurt female participants and impair their development. (As we shall see later, some children begin the practice of gymnastics around age five).

At a meeting with *Washington Post* editors and reporters on September 30, 1992, Harvey Schiller, U. S. Olympic Committee Executive Director, stated that, "It is incumbent on us that we advance the issues of science and technology in this area." And further, "Even before the Games, we had discussions with medical people, including some with specialties in obstetrics and gynecology, about perhaps doing some studies on young women involved in sports." It is interesting to note that this issue was not raised by athletes, coaches, or sports administrators, but by the public in letters and other forums.

For over 40 years some critics have been concerned with possible injuries that children might sustain in *contact* sports, especially football. This concern has centered around the notion that too much pressure would be applied to the *epiphyses,* particularly in such activities as football.

In the long bones there is first a center of ossification for the bone called the *diaphysis* and one or more centers for each extremity called the *epiphyses.* Ossification proceeds from the diaphysis toward the epiphysis, and from the epiphysis toward the diaphysis. As each new portion is ossified thin layers of cartilage continue to develop between the diaphysis and epiphysis and during this period of growth, these outstrip ossification. When this ceases the growth of the bone stops. Injury can occur as a result of trauma which could be due to a "blow" incurred in a contact sport.

If we are to be successful in our efforts to avoid injuries to child sports participants, more emphasis needs to be exerted in the direction of preventive measures. Such measures can be taken by those who have the direct responsibility of working with children in sports activities. And this is the subject of the ensuing section of the chapter.

SUPERVISION OF CHILDREN'S SPORTS

In the present context, the term *supervision* is essentially concerned with those persons who *coach* or *manage* children's sports teams. I am frequently asked by parents about the advisability of their children's participation in sports. My immediate response is to "check out" the qualifications and objectives of those persons who will assume the responsibility for coaching.

At one time this was a much more serious matter because some coaches had little experience—especially in how to deal with growing children in competitive situations.

At the present time, however, this situation has been alleviated appreciably, mainly because of such organizations as the *National Youth Sports Coaches Association* (NYSCA). This is a nonprofit association that has proven to be a frontrunner in the development of a national training system for volunteer sports youth coaches.

One of my former students, Fred Engh, is the Association's President/CEO and he has provided me with materials, some of which I would like to pass on to the reader.

To date, almost 450,000 coaches have undertaken the NYSCA's three-year, three-level program to qualify for membership and certification. This certification program focuses on helping volunteer coaches understand the psychological, physical, and emotional impact they have on children age 6 to 12. The criteria for NYSCA certification and membership are reviewed by the NYSCA National Executive Board which is comprised of representatives from the fields of education, recreation, and sports law.

One of the important aspects of the NYSCA is the following "Coaches' Code of Ethics."

- I hereby pledge to live up to my certification as a NYSCA Coach by following the NYSCA Code of Ethics.
- I will place the emotional and physical well-being of my players ahead of any personal desire to win.
- I will remember to treat each player as an individual, remembering the large spread of emotional and physical development for the same age group.
- I will do my very best to provide a safe play situation for my players.
- I promise to review and practice the necessary first aid principles needed to treat injuries of my players.
- I will do my best to organize practices that are fun and challenging for all my players.
- I will lead, by example, in demonstrating fair play and sportsmanship to all my players.
- I will insure that I am knowledgeable in the rules of each sport that I coach, and that I will teach these rules to my players.
- I will use those coaching techniques appropriate for each of the skills that I teach.

- I will remember that I am a youth coach, and that the game is for children and not adults.

One of the problems with children's sports has been the attitude of some parents who seem to exhibit "parental pride in the parent" rather than "parental pride in the child." Aware of this, the NYSCA has developed the following "Parents' Code of Ethics."

- I hereby pledge to provide positive support, care and encouragement for my child participating in youth sports by following this Code of Ethics.
- I will encourage good sportsmanship by demonstrating positive support for all players, coaches, and officials at every game, practice or other youth sports event.
- I will place the emotional and physical well-being of my child ahead of any personal desire to win.
- I will insist that my child plays in a safe and healthy environment.
- I will provide support for coaches and officials working with my child to provide a positive, enjoyable experience for all.
- I will demand a drug-, alcohol- and tobacco-free sports environment for my child and agree to assist by refraining from their use at all youth sports events.
- I will remember that the game is for the children and not for adults.
- I will do my very best to make youth sports fun for my child.
- I will ask my child to treat other players, coaches, fans, and officials with respect regardless of race, sex, creed, or ability.
- I will promise to help my child enjoy the youth sports experience within my personal constraints by assisting with coaching, being a respectful fan, providing transportation or whatever I am capable of doing.
- I will require that my child's coach be trained in the responsibilities of being a youth sports coach and that the coach agree to the youth sports Coaches' Code of Ethics.
- I will read the NYSCA National Standards for Youth Sports and do everything in my power to assist all youth sports organizations to implement and enforce them.

_____   _____   _____
Parent Signature   *Parent Signature*   *Date*

(NYSCA is located at 2611 Old Okeechobee Road, West Palm Beach, Florida, 33409.)

Little League Baseball, Inc. also provides important information for its managers. Following are some highlights from the publication, "The Other Side—A Manager's Guide to Working with Little Leaguers."

1. Managing in Little League involves more than just knowing baseball or softball. Much more. To transform a group of young individuals into a team playing together is a challenge. Even the most knowledgeable ballplayer cannot expect to be successful without knowing how to deal with kids. As one assumes the role of a Little League manager or coach, he or she becomes parent, psychologist, referee, minister, best friend—and baseball instructor.

2. Managing in Little League is not a self-serving recreation. One must be in tune with the best interests of the players' welfare. Nothing is right unless it is for their good. Managing is a volunteer service through which players can be supervised and guided while participating in Little League.

3. Not everyone is meant to be a manager in Little League. The basic attributes that are fundamental to working with others come easy to some. The techniques of teaching the basics of playing ball can be acquired through study, while the talent to handle the personal relationships of team management lies partly within one's personality. In some there is an inherent ability to getting along with youngsters. Do you have this ability?

4. Youngsters are naturally restless and in need of activity. This restlessness is not their own way of agitating—they are just being themselves. Attention spans are short, so be brief and to the point when talking and demonstrating the techniques of playing ball. Remember that children are not adults and cannot be expected to conform to adult standards of behavior. Keep practices short, peppy and above all, keep everyone busy.

5. Be lavish with praise and compassion. Your players respond best to you when you respond to them. You will experience the pleasure of being an important element in the social, as well as athletic development of your players.

Little League also publishes the following pamphlets for its managers. *Little League Training Handbook, My Coach Says, Little League Rules in Pictures, Care and Conditioning of the Pitching Arm,* and *Play it Safe.* (Little League Baseball, Inc. is located at Box 3485, Williamsport, Pennsylvania, 17701.)

The extent to which coaches and managers of children's sports teams practice the above principles is difficult to determine. I would like to think that the great majority of them make a serious effort to do so. Unfortunately, the media seems to be more concerned with placing emphasis on news that is confrontational and scandalous rather than those factors of a positive nature. Thus, we are more likely to read or hear about the coach who "slashed a rival coach's throat with a penknife" or the manager who was "clubbed with a bat by a rival manager" than we are to be informed about the coach who has nothing but the best interest of the children in mind.

With regard to the latter, the results of a recent study[7] are most encouraging. The UCLA Sports Psychology Laboratory studied the attitudes of 2,000 Southern California boys and girls who participate in sports and found that the factor that contributed most to their enjoyment was "positive coach support."

---

[7]Sewell, Dan, Are Parents Ruining the Game?, West Palm Beach, Florida, *Youth Sports Coach,* Fall 1992.

My own extensive surveys of children's sports participants on this subject have yielded some interesting results.

On a scale with 4.0 being the highest, boys rated their coaches at 3.4 and girls gave their coaches a 3.3 rating.

In answer to the question, "What do you like *best* about your coach?" boys gave the following most prominent answers.

The coach:

- is nice (34%)
- is fair (26%)
- teaches us good things (26%)
- is funny (7%)
- says it is all right if we lose (7%)

Girls gave the following answers to this question.
The coach:

- is nice (42%)
- is funny (28%)
- is fair (14%)
- helps us to play better (10%)
- is young (6%)

In answer to the question "What do you like *least* about your coach?" boys answered as follows.

The coach:

- gets mad and yells at us (64%)
- works us too hard (22%)
- doesn't let me play enough (8%)
- is not a good teacher (3%)
- doesn't praise us enough (3%)

Girls answered this question as follows.
The coach:

- gets mad and yells at us (57%)
- doesn't teach us much (19%)
- work us too hard (14%)
- doesn't praise us enough (5%)
- seems unhappy (5%)

In attempting to verbalize all of these data, one could come up with all sorts of possibilities of how children characterize their coach. Here is one such possibility. *The coach is usually a nice person with a sense of humor who is generally fair, but at the same time one who is likely to get mad and yell at the players.*

There is no question about it, the quality level of supervision is an important factor in children's sports. However, in the final analysis the success or failure of any program will ultimately depend upon its contribution to the total development of the child—and this is the subject that is introduced in the following chapter.

I have one final note in closing this introductory chapter. At the beginning of the chapter I gave as a working definition of the term *children:* "boys and girls through the chronological age of 12." In closing the chapter it might be interesting to consider the age at which some children first become involved in sports.

It seems that more and more emphasis is being placed on "very tiny tots." Beginning some years ago, the "water babies" program which is concerned with teaching infants to swim is said to have met with some success.

In the mid 1970s the infant exercise concept prompted widespread interest. One such program call *Gymboree* was started in 1976 by Joan Barnes, a former dance instructor from Burlingame, California. This program is divided into three sessions according to a child's age: (1) *Baby Gym*—for infants three months to one year with parents helping their children with choreographical exercises such as bicycling legs or stretching arms; (2) *Gymboree*—for children from one year to 18 months with time devoted to "free exploration" and some structured time for songs, fingerplay and creative movements, and (3) *Gym Grad*—for preschoolers two and one half to four years of age using "gymberexercises," a combination of stretches, body awareness and aerobics and following a different theme each week.

When the former East Bloc communist countries were having so much success in olympic gymnastics it was attributed to starting early in life—as early as age five. The recent success of American olympic gymnasts, particularly girls, is said to be a result of starting at a very early age.

The same could be said for American olympic swimmers. In a television interview with one of the parents of an olympic medalist, he reported that she could swim the "length of the pool" at the age of 18 months.

Finally, the previously-mentioned Davis and Isaacs cite the case of the four-year-old holding an age group record for running the marathon (26 plus miles) in six hours and three seconds. They also mention that there have been attempts to conduct an "Infant Olympics." And, in the near future (maybe or maybe not facetiously) there may be national and international records for *creeping* and *crawling.* In fact, believe it or not, a national championship crawling contest for infants under 18 months of age, was held in Dallas, Texas on November 26, 1992.

It should be mentioned that this trend toward involvement of children in sports at a very early age is causing a great deal of concern among many pediatricians and child development specialists.

Chapter 2

CHILD DEVELOPMENT AND SPORTS

I f we accept the idea that sports participation for children should be a worthwhile educational experience, we need to consider the purpose of education for children.

When we analyze the various statements of the purposes of education for children which have been made by responsible educational agencies and groups, it is a relatively easy matter to identify a constantly emerging pattern. These statements through the years have gradually evolved into a more or less general agreement among present-day childhood educational leaders that the goal of education for children is to stimulate and guide the development of them so that they will function in life activities involving vocation, citizenship, and enriched leisure; and further, so that they will possess as high a level of physical, social, emotional, and intellectual well-being as each one's individual capacity will permit. More succinctly stated, the purpose of education for children in our modern society should be in the direction of *total development* of the child.

The ensuing sections of this chapter should be read with this general frame of reference in mind. This is to say that if it is a valid assumption that the purpose of education for children is to attempt to assure their total development, then it is incumbent upon us to explore the developmental processes as they relate to children's sports. This chapter will overview generally these processes as they apply to sports, and Chapters 3 through 6 will go into detail on each of the developmental processes as they relate to children's sports.

When it is considered that development of children brings about needs, and that these needs must be met satisfactorily, the importance of an understanding of development is readily discerned. When understanding the various aspects of development is accomplished, one is then in a better position to provide improved procedures for meeting the needs of each individual child. This implies that we might be guided by what could be called a developmental philosophy if we are to meet with

19

any degree of success in our dealings with children in their sports participation.

THE MEANING OF DEVELOPMENT

As mentioned previously, total development is the fundamental purpose of the education of children. All attempts at such education should take into account a combination of *physical, social, emotional,* and *intellectual* aspects of human behavior. In fact, a long standing definition states that *child development is an interdisciplinary approach to the study of children, drawing upon such sciences as biology, physiology, embryology, pediatrics, sociology, psychiatry, anthropology, and psychology; emphasis is placed on the importance of understanding children through study of their mental, emotional, social, and physical growth; particular emphasis is laid on the appraisal of the impacts of the growing personality of home, school, and community.*[1]

The forms of development that I will consider are the physical, social, emotional, and intellectual aspects. Of course, there are other forms of development, but perhaps they can be subclassified under one of the above areas. For example, *motor development,* which has been defined as a progressive change in motor performance, is considered as a part of the broader aspect of *physical development.* In addition, *moral development,* which is concerned with the capacity of the child to distinguish between standards of right and wrong could be considered as a dimension of the broader aspect of *social development.* This is to say that moral development involving achievement in ability to determine right from wrong is influential in the child's social behavior.

A great deal of clinical and experimental evidence indicates that a human being must be considered as a whole and not a collection of parts. For purposes here, I would prefer to use the term *total personality* in referring to the child as a unified individual or total being. Perhaps a more common term is *whole child.* When we consider personality from a point of man existing as a person, it is interesting to note that "existence as a person" is one rather common definition of personality.

The total personality consists of the sum of all of the physical, social, emotional, and intellectual aspects of any individual, that is, the major forms of development previously identified. The total personality is "one thing" comprising these various major aspects. All of these compo-

---

[1]Good, Carter, *Dictionary of Education,* 2nd ed., New York, McGraw-Hill, 1959.

nents are highly interrelated and interdependent as depicted in Figure 1. The four aspects of personality are interrelated and interdependent with the child's total development and sports participation as shown by the overlapping circles. Each component, although a system in and of itself, is related to and influences a larger entity, namely the total personality of the child and has implications for children's sports.

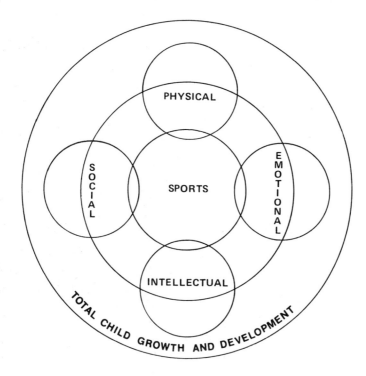

Figure 1.

All of the aspects of total personality are important to the balance and health of the total personality, because only in terms of their health can the personality as a whole maintain a completely healthy state. The condition of any one aspect affects another to a degree and thus, the personality as a whole.

When a nervous child stutters or becomes nauseated, a mental state is *not* necessarily causing a physical symptom. On the contrary, a pressure imposed upon the organism causes a series of reactions, which include, thought, verbalization, digestive processes, and muscular function. It is not that the mind causes the body to become upset; the total organism is upset by a situation and reflects its upset in several ways, including disturbance in thought, feeling, and bodily processes. The whole individual responds in interaction with the social and physical environment; and, as the child is affected by the environment, he or she in turn, has an effect upon it.

However, because of long tradition during which physical development *or* intellectual development, rather than physical *and* intellectual development, has been glorified, we oftentimes are still accustomed to dividing the two in our thinking. The result may be that we sometimes pull human beings apart with this kind of thinking.

Traditional attitudes that separate the mind and body tend to lead to unbalanced development of the child with respect to mind and body and/or social adjustment. What is more unfortunate is that we fail to utilize the strengths of one to serve the needs of the other. To better understand the concept of total personality in the human organism, a schematic diagram of the total personality is seen in Figure 2.

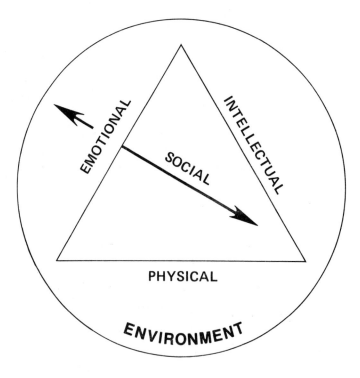

Figure 2.

The circle is the total environment of the child that circumscribes and confines all aspects of the total personality. The triangle—with its three sides—physical, emotional, and intellectual aspects of total personality form a single figure with the *physical* aspect as a base. An arrow extending from the center of the triangle upwards through one of its sides is designated *social* to represent interpersonal relationships within the field of the child and his environment. The arrow is pointed at both ends to suggest a two-way process. The child is affected by those around him or her and the child affects them (largely through language as a means of communication). The triangle is dependent upon a balance of all its parts, and if one part of the triangle is changed the entire triangle is reshaped. It is interesting to draw diagrams in which one after the other of the sides is shortened—as in one kind or another of developmental failure or retardation—and see how this affects the triangle. It is also interesting to make personal applications such as the following: "What happens to my intellectual performance when I am worried or have a stomachache?" "What changes occur in my body when I 'feel' frightened, embarassed, or angered?" Obviously, similar applications can be made to children.

The foregoing statements have attempted to point out rather forcefully the idea that the identified components of the total personality comprise the unified individual. The fact that each of these aspects might well be considered as a separate entity should also be taken into account. As such, each aspect should warrant a separate discussion. This appears extremely important if one is to understand fully the place of each aspect as an integral part of the whole personality. The following discussion of the physical, social, emotional, and intellectual aspects of personality as they relate to sports for children should be viewed in this general frame of reference.

THE PHYSICAL ASPECT OF PERSONALITY

One point of departure in discussing the physical aspect of personality could be to state that "everybody has a body." Some are short, some are tall, some are lean, and some are fat. Children come in different sizes, but all of them have a certain innate capacity that is influenced by the environment.

It might be said of the child that he "is" his body. It is something he can see. It is his base of operation—what was previously referred to as the "physical base." The other components of the total personality—social, emotional, and intellectual are somewhat vague as far as the child is concerned. Although these are manifested in various ways, children do not always see them as they do the physical aspect. Consequently, it becomes ever more important that a child be helped early in life to gain control over the physical aspect, or what is known as *basic body control.* The ability to do this, of course, will vary from one child to another. It will likely depend upon the status of physical fitness of the child. The broad area of physical fitness can be broken down into certain components, and it is important that children achieve to the best of their natural ability with these components. There is not complete agreement though of the identification of these components of physical fitness. However, the President's Council on Physical Fitness and Sports considers these components to consist of muscular strength, endurance, and power; circulatory-respiratory endurance; agility; speed; flexibility; balance; and coordination. (These components will be discussed in detail in the following chapter.)

The components of physical fitness and thus, the physical aspect of personality can be measured by calibrated instruments, such as measurements of muscular strength. Moreover, we can tell how tall a child is or how heavy he or she is at any stage of his or her development. In addition, other accurate data can be derived with assessments of blood pressure, blood counts, urinalysis, and the like.

THE SOCIAL ASPECT OF PERSONALITY

Human beings are social beings. They work together for the benefit of society. They have fought together in time of national emergencies in order to preserve the kind of society they believe in and they play together. While all this may be true, the social aspect of personality is still quite vague and confusing, particularly where children are concerned.

It was a relatively easy matter to identify certain components of physical fitness such as strength, endurance, and the like. However, this does not necessarily hold true for components of social fitness. The components of physical fitness are the same for children as for adults. On the other hand, the components of social fitness for children may be different from the components of social fitness for adults. By some adult standards children might be considered as social misfits because certain behavior of children might not be socially acceptable to some adults. This is conversely true as well.

To the chagrin of some adults, young children are uninhibited in the social aspect of their personality development. In this regard, we need to be concerned with social maturity as it pertains to the growing and ever-changing child. This is to say that we need to give consideration to certain characteristics of social maturity and how well they are dealt with at the different stages of child development.

As children participate in sports, perhaps we need to ask ourselves such questions as, "Are we helping children to become self-reliant by giving them independence at the proper time? Are we helping them to be outgoing and interested in others as well as themselves? Are we helping them to know how to satisfy their own needs in a socially desirable way? Are we helping them to develop a wholesome attitude toward themselves and others?

THE EMOTIONAL ASPECT OF PERSONALITY

In introducing the subject of emotion, we are confronted with the fact that for many years it has been a difficult concept to define, and, in addition, there have been many changing ideas and theories in the study of emotion.

Obviously, it is not the purpose of a book of this nature to attempt to go into any great depth on a subject that has been one of the most intricate undertakings of psychology for many years. A few general statements relative to the nature of emotion do appear to be in order, however, if we are to understand more clearly this aspect of personality as it concerns children's sports.

Emotion may be defined as *a response the body makes to a stimulus for which it is not prepared or which suggests a possible source of gain or loss for him or her.* For example, if a child is confronted with a situation and does not have a satisfactory response, the emotional pattern of fear may result. If one finds himself or herself in a position where desires are frustrated, the emotional pattern of anger may occur.

This line of thought suggests that emotions might be classified in two different ways: those that are pleasant and those that are unpleasant. For example, joy could be considered a pleasant emotional experience while fear would be an unpleasant one. It is interesting to note that a good proportion of the literature is devoted to emotions that are unpleasant. It has been found that in psychology books much more space is given to such emotional patterns as fear, hate, guilt, and anxiety than the such pleasant emotions as love, sympathy, and contentment.

Generally speaking, the pleasantness or unpleasantness of an emotion seems to be determined by its strength or intensity, by the nature of the situation arousing it, and by the way an individual perceives or interprets the situation. The emotions of children tend to be more intense than those of adults. If an adult is not aware of this aspect of child behavior, he or she will not likely understand why a child may react rather violently to a situation that to an adult seems somewhat insignificant. The fact that different children will react differently to the same type of situation also should be taken into account. For example, something that might anger one child might have a rather passive influence on another child. In this regard, it is interesting to observe the effect that winning or losing has on certain children.

THE INTELLECTUAL ASPECT OF PERSONALITY

The word "intelligence" is derived from the Latin word *intellectus,* which literally means the "power of knowing." Intelligence has been defined in many ways. One general definition of it is *the capacity to learn or understand.*

Individuals possess varying degrees of intelligence, and most people fall within a range of what is called "normal" intelligence. In dealing with this aspect of the personality we should perhaps give attention to what might be considered as some components of intellectual fitness. However, this is a difficult thing to do. Because of the somewhat nebulous nature of intelligence, it is practically impossible to identify specific components of it. Thus, we need to view intellectual fitness in a somewhat different manner.

For purposes of this discussion, I would like to consider intellectual fitness from two different, but closely related points of view: first, from a standpoint of intellectual needs, and second, from a standpoint of how certain things influence intelligence. It might be said that if a child's intellectual needs are being met, then perhaps we could also say that he or she is intellectually fit. From the second point of view, if we know how certain things influence intelligence then we might understand better how to contribute to intellectual fitness by improving upon some of these factors.

There appears to be some rather general agreement with regard to the intellectual needs of children. Among others, these needs include (1) a need for challenging experiences at the child's level of ability, (2) a need for intellectually successful and satisfying experiences, (3) a need for the opportunity to solve problems, and (4) a need for the opportunity to participate in creative experiences instead of always having to conform. Some of the factors that tend to influence intelligence are (1) health and physical condition, (2) emotional disturbance, and (3) certain social and economic factors. When adults have a realization of the intellectual needs and factors influencing intelligence, perhaps then and only then can they deal satisfactorily with children in helping them in their intellectual pursuits.

TOTAL DEVELOPMENT AND OBJECTIVES OF SPORTS FOR CHILDREN

The component elements of total development can satisfactorily emerge as valid sports objectives for children. These elements have been expressed in terms of physical, social, emotional, and intellectual development comprising the total personality. As such, they can logically become the physical, social, emotional, and intellectual objectives of sports for children.

The term *objective* appears to have been adopted by education from the military. The latter uses it to identify areas to be assaulted and/or captured in some way. The *Dictionary of Education* gives the following definition of the term as *aim, end in view, or purpose of a course of action or a belief; that which is anticipated as desirable in the early phases of an activity and serves to select, regulate, and direct later aspects of the act so that the total process is designed and integrated.* Various other terms are used to convey the same meaning. Some of these include *aim, goal,* and *purpose.* Regardless of the particular terms used, we might well consider it with regard to a very simple meaning; that is, what should we be trying to accomplish through the sports medium where total development of children is concerned?

PHYSICAL OBJECTIVES OF CHILDREN'S SPORTS

It may be stated generally that a good program of sports for children can be considered as a stimulant to physical growth. Moreover, the general consensus indicates that participation in a well-balanced sports program could be a good way of maintaining optimum health.

It should be kept in mind that some children have great physical advantages simply because of the particular body build they may happen to have, and others may be at a relatively great disadvantage because of a very heavyset, or slight body build. Consequently, our objective should not be to make *every* child a great athlete. Rather, the physical objectives must be to help *each* child who participates to develop his or her individual potentialities for controlled and effective body movement as fully as possible.

Two major objectives emerge out of the physical aspect of personality. The first of these takes into account *maintaining a suitable level of physical fitness,* and, second, there is the consideration of the *development of skill and ability.*

Maintaining a Suitable Level of Physical Fitness

Physical fitness presupposes an adequate intake of good food and an adequate amount of rest and sleep, but beyond these things, activity involving all the big muscles of the body is essential. Just how high a level of physical fitness should be maintained from one stage of life to another is a difficult question to answer, because we must raise the question: "Fitness for what?"

Physical fitness has been perceived in different ways by different people. However, when all of these descriptions are put together, it is likely that they will be characterized more by their similarities than by their differences. For purposes here, let us think of physical fitness as the level of ability of the human organism to perform certain physical tasks; or, put another way, the fitness to perform various specified tasks requiring muscular effort.

A reasonable question to raise at this point is: "Why is a reasonably high level of physical fitness desirable in modern times when there are so many effort-saving devices available that for many people strenuous activity is really not necessary anymore?" One possible answer to this is because all of us stand at the end of a long line of ancestors, all of whom at least lived long enough to have children. They were fit and vigorous and strong enough to survive in the face of savage beasts and savage men, in addition to hard work. Only the fit survived. Not very far back in your own family tree you would find people who had to be rugged and extremely active in order to live. Vigorous action and physical ruggedness are our biological heritage. Possibly, because of the kind of background that we have, our bodies simply function better when we are active.

Most child development specialists agree that vigorous play in childhood is essential for the satisfactory growth of the various organs and systems of the body. It has been said that "play is the business of childhood." To conduct this "business" successfully and happily, the child should be physically fit. Good nutrition, rest, and properly conducted sports programs have the potential to do much to develop and maintain the physical fitness of children.

Development of Skill and Ability

The second major physical objective of children's sports has to do with disciplined bodily movement. The physically educated child, commensurate with his or her capacity and within his or her own limitations, is adept in a variety of sports activities. Children enjoy those activities in which they are reasonably proficient. Thus, we are dealing with an important principle related to our children's sports objectives; that is, if children are to enjoy participating in sports activities, they need to be reasonably competent in the skills involved in these activities. Consequently, there must be objectives both in terms of the number of skills to which children at the different age levels are introduced and the level of competence to be achieved at that age level so that they may associate a pleasurable experience with participation. (Chapter 7 will be devoted to sports skills for children.)

We must reckon with another matter that is closely related to competence in a wide variety of skills. Some organizations have stressed the very strenuous team sports in their programs and others have placed emphasis on what have been called "lifetime sports" that may be used in later life. A sensible point of view on this subject would appear to be that we should develop competence in a variety of skills for use "now *and* in the future." Stated more specifically, as an objective of children's sports it could be said that all children should be prepared by their sports experience to participate in suitable and satisfying activities for use now and in the future. Those individuals who would place undue emphasis on strenuous and violent activities at the expense of lifetime activities for use in the future should pay special attention to the word "suitable" in the previous sentence. What is suitable during one period of life is not necessarily suitable during another. The intensely competitive, vigorous— and in some cases—violent sports are considered by some not to be suitable, especially for young children.

In summary, the physical objective of children's sports should imply organic development commensurate with vigor, vitality, strength, balance, flexibility, and neuromuscular coordination, together with the development of skill and ability in a variety of activities for use now and in the future.

SOCIAL OBJECTIVES OF CHILDREN'S SPORTS

The sports "laboratory" (areas where activities take place) should present near ideal surroundings and environment for the social development of children. Why are people who are in the field of children's sports convinced that this area provides some of the very best means for teaching vital social skills? By their very nature, sports activities are essentially socially oriented. If any type of sports experience is to be successful and satisfying, the children involved must possess or acquire considerable skill in dealing with one another. They must learn to work together for the interest of the group. They must learn to accept and respect the rules of the games that they play. They must learn that sometimes it is necessary to place the welfare of the group ahead of their own personal desires. They must respect the rights of others. They must think and plan with the group and for the group. They must learn to win and lose gracefully.

In looking back over this list of social skills that is important in children's sports, it should be discerned that it is just such social skills that are necessary for happy and successful social living everywhere. A qualified children's sports coach or manager should find numerous opportunities to develop skills of interpersonal relationships that far exceed the basic essentials for successful play. Indeed, successful children's sports coaches and managers should consider the development of increased social awareness and social skills as important objectives of their programs, and they should make specific plans to reach these objectives. They should recognize that children's sports can have a profoundly humanizing effect upon children; participants quickly learn to evaluate their team members on the basis of what they can do and what kinds of persons they are rather than on the basis of their looks, race, religion, color, or economic status.

A brief summary of the social objective of children's sports might imply satisfactory experiences on how to meet and get along with others, development of proper attitudes toward one's peers, and the development of a sense of social values.

EMOTIONAL OBJECTIVES OF CHILDREN'S SPORTS

Most everyone recognizes that some sports experiences can be highly emotionalized situations. For the child, there is the excitement that may be felt before certain kinds of sports activities are initiated. When play is in progress, there is the thrill of making skillful moves and the possible disappointments or frustrations when one does not do well. Finally, the after-play emotions, determined to some extent by how well the child performed in relation to how well he or she thinks they can perform, but in almost all instances the pleasurable emotions caused by the good feeling that the time has been well spent.

With regard to the foregoing comments, the results of my surveys are of interest. Forty percent of the boys and 37 percent of the girls reported that they were "very nervous" before a game. Moreover, 31 percent of the boys and 17 percent of the girls felt pressure to win from their parents and/or coaches.

In answer to the question: "How do you feel when you win?" boys replied as follows.

- Good (42%)
- Happy (38%)
- Great (18%)
- Like I did my best (2%)

Girls essentially displayed the same pleasant emotions with the following answers.

- Happy (41%)
- Good (40%)
- Great (16%)
- OK (3%)

To the question: "How do you feel when you lose?" boys answered as follows.

- Bad (32%)
- Sad (16%)
- OK (16%)
- No feelings (9%)
- Fine (7%)
- Unhappy (7%)
- Good (6%)

- Like I want to kill myself (5%)
- Disgusted (2%)

In answer to this question, girls expressed some of the same unpleasant emotions as the boys, but for the most part, they did not find losing as distressful as witnessed by the largest percentage feeling "OK" about it.

- OK (33%)
- Bad (24%)
- Sad (16%)
- Mad (7%)
- Upset (5%)
- Great (3%)
- Good (2%)
- Unhappy (2%)
- No feelings (2%)
- Disappointed (2%)
- Stupid (1%)
- Embarrassed (1%)
- Dumb (1%)
- Fine (1%)

From the point of view of children's sports objectives, there are two very important things that might well be accomplished with the emotional aspect of personality. These may be classified as (1) to provide for fun and satisfying emotional release, and (2) to develop in children an increased capacity to control their emotions, thus contributing to the development of emotional maturity.

Fun and Emotional Release

Certainly one of the most important objectives of children's sports should be wholesome fun. Moreover, it is a desirable objective of children's sports to provide opportunities for children to enjoy uninhibited and vigorous movement. Because of their very nature, children require vigorous activity for proper growth and development. *They should not sit and watch television for prolonged periods without such activity!* (But many of them do, however.)

Children's sports should be primarily a learning experience for children, but their value as a means of easing emotional tensions in the form of genuine fun certainly should not be underestimated. My studies show that 53 percent of the girls and 48 percent of the boys participate in children's sports because of the fun they derive from them.

Emotional Control

It could be said that the major difference between a so-called "normal" individual and an incorrigible one is that the former has the ability to control his or her emotional impulses to a greater extent than the latter. Perhaps all of us at one time or another have experienced the same kind of emotions that have led the abnormal individual to commit violence, but we have been able to hold our powerful and violent emotions in check. This may be an extreme example, but it should suggest something of the importance of emotional control in modern society.

It would appear that a reasonable and natural objective of children's sports should be to help children increase their capacity to handle and control their emotions. The thoughtful coach or manager is aware of opportunities offered in play situations for children to learn to deal with their emotional arousals in socially acceptable ways. He or she helps to guide children in such a way that they learn to take pride in their ability to restrain themselves when necessary in order to abide by the rules of fair play and to behave like reasonable and decent human beings. The coach or manager has real emotionally charged situations with which to work in order to teach children to deal with their strong emotions.

Another aspect of controlling the emotions is becoming able to function effectively and intelligently in an emotionally charged situation. Sometimes success in children's sports experiences may hinge upon this ability, as does success in many other life situations. Extremes of emotional upset must be avoided if the child is to be able to think and act effectively. In sports situations, children should learn that if they immediately put their minds to work on other things, such as group cooperation, they can then control their emotions.

In summarizing the emotional objective of children's sports, it could be said that it should be implied that sympathetic guidance should be provided in meeting anxieties, joys, and sorrows, and help should be given in developing aspirations, affections, and security.

INTELLECTUAL OBJECTIVES OF CHILDREN'S SPORTS

Of the contributions that children's sports might make to the development of total personality, the one concerned with intellectual development has been subjected to a great deal of criticism by some individuals. However, sports are not "all brawn and no brain" activities. Close scrutiny of the possibilities of intellectual development through children's sports reveals, however, that a very desirable contribution can be made through this medium. This belief is substantiated in part by the affirmations made by many prominent philosophers and educators over a long period of years.

In a well-planned sports experience, there are numerous opportunities to exercise judgment and resort to reflective thinking in the solution of various kinds of problems. In addition, in a well-balanced program, children must acquire a knowledge of certain rules and regulations in the games that they play. It is also essential for effective participation that children gain an understanding of the various fundamentals and strategy involved in the performance of certain kinds of sports activities. As will be seen in Chapter 6, there are certain aspects of some children's sports that involve improvement of the various forms of perception.

A brief summary of the intellectual objective of children's sports implies the development of specific knowledge pertaining to rules, regulations, and strategies involved in a variety of worthwhile sports experiences. In addition, this objective should be concerned with the value of children's sports as a most worthwhile learning medium in the development of certain intellectual concepts and understandings.

It has been the purpose of this chapter to present an overview of child development, focusing upon the interdependence and interrelationship of the various components of the total personality. Chapters 3 through 6 will go into detail on each of these components with emphasis upon the potential each has for child development through sports.

Chapter 3

PHYSICAL DEVELOPMENT OF CHILDREN THROUGH SPORTS

Physical development is concerned with the child's physical ability to function at an increasingly higher level. For example, a stage of development in the infant is from creeping to crawling. This is later followed by the developmental stage of walking when the child moves to an upright position and begins to move over the surface area by putting one foot in front of the other.

PHYSICAL NEEDS OF CHILDREN

If any physical values are to accrue from children's sports, it becomes imperative that such sports be planned on the basis of the physical needs of children. These needs are reflected in the physical developmental characteristics of growing children. Many such characteristics are identified in the following lists of the different age levels.

This list of physical characteristics, as well as the lists of social, emotional, and intellectual characteristics, which will appear in subsequent chapters, have been developed through a documentary analysis of over a score of sources that have appeared in the literature on child development over the years. It should be understood that these characteristics are suggestive of the behavior patterns of the so-called "normal" child. This implies that if a child does not conform to these characteristics, it should not be interpreted to mean that he or she is seriously deviating from the normal. In other words, it should be recognized that each child progresses at his or her own rate and that there can be overlapping of the characteristics for each of the age levels. In examining these lists, adults should attempt to determine the extent to which a given sport *contributes* or *detracts* from them.

Five-Year-Old Children

1. Boys' height, 42 to 46 inches; weight, 38 to 49 pounds; girls' height, 42 to 46 inches; weight, 36 to 48 pounds.
2. May grow two or three inches and gain from three to six pounds during the year.
3. Girls may be about a year ahead of boys in physiological development.
4. Beginning to have better control of body.
5. The large muscles are better developed than the small muscles that control the fingers and hands.
6. Usually determined whether he or she will be right- or left-handed.
7. Eye and hand coordination is not complete.
8. May have farsighted vision.
9. Vigorous and noisy, but activity appears to have definite direction.
10. Tires easily and needs plenty of rest.

Six-Year-Old Children

1. Boys' height, 44 to 48 inches; weight 41 to 54 pounds; girls' height, 43 to 48 inches; weight, 40 to 53 pounds.
2. Growth is gradual in weight and height.
3. Good supply of energy.
4. Marked activity urge absorbs the child in running, jumping, chasing, and dodging games.
5. Muscular control becoming more effective with large objects.
6. There is a noticeable change in the eye-hand behavior.
7. Legs lengthening rapidly.
8. Big muscles crave activity.

Seven-Year-Old Children

1. Boys' height, 46 to 51 inches; weight, 45 to 60 pounds; girls' height, 46 to 50 inches; weight, 44 to 59 pounds.
2. Big muscle activity predominates in interest and value.
3. More improvement in eye-hand coordination.
4. May grow two or three inches and gain three to five pounds in weight during the year.
5. Tires easily and shows fatigue in the afternoon.
6. Has slow reaction time.
7. Heart and lungs are smallest in proportion to body size.

8. General health may be precarious, with susceptibility to disease high and resistance low.
9. Endurance relatively low.
10. Coordination is improving with throwing, and catching becoming more accurate.
11. Whole-body movements are under better control.
12. Small accessory muscles developing.
13. Displays amazing amounts of vitality.

Eight-Year-Old Children

1. Boys' height, 48 to 53 inches; weight, 49 to 70 pounds; girls' height, 48 to 52 inches; weight, 47 to 66 pounds.
2. Interested in games requiring coordination of small muscles.
3. Arms are lengthening and hands are growing larger.
4. Eyes can accommodate more easily.
5. Some develop poor posture.
6. Accidents appear to occur more frequently at this age.
7. Appreciates correct skill performance.

Nine-Year-Old Children

1. Boys' height, 50 to 55 inches; weight, 55 to 74 pounds; girls' height, 50 to 54 inches; weight, 52 to 74 pounds.
2. Increasing strength in arms, hands and fingers.
3. Endurance improving.
4. Needs and enjoys much activity; boys like to shout, wrestle, and tussle with each other.
5. A few girls near puberty.
6. Girls gaining growth maturity up to two years over boys.
7. Girls enjoy active group games, but are usually less noisy and less full of spontaneous energy than boys.
8. Likely to slouch and assume unusual postures.
9. Eyes are much better developed and are able to accommodate to close work with less strain.
10. May tend to overexercise.
11. Sex differences appear in recreational activities.
12. Interested in own body and wants to have questions answered.

Ten-Year-Old Children

1. Boys' height, 52 to 57 inches; weight, 59 to 82 pounds; girls' height, 52 to 57 inches; weight 57 to 83 pounds.
2. Individuality is well-defined, and insights are more mature.
3. Stability in growth rate and stability of physiological processes.
4. Physically active and likes to rush around and be busy.
5. Before the onset of puberty there is usually a resting period or plateau, during which the boy or girl does not appear to gain in either height or weight.
6. Interested in the development of more skills.
7. Reaction time is improving.
8. Muscular strength does not seem to keep pace with growth.
9. Refining and elaborating skill in the use of small muscles.

Eleven-Year-Old Children

1. Boys' height, 53 to 58 inches; weight 64 to 91 pounds; girls' height, 53 to 59 inches; weight 64 to 95 pounds.
2. Marked changes in muscle system causing awkwardness and habits sometimes distressing to the child.
3. Shows fatigue more easily.
4. Some girls and a few boys suddenly show rapid growth and evidence of the approach of adolescence.
5. On the average, girls may be taller and heavier than boys.
6. Uneven growth of different parts of the body.
7. Rapid growth may result in laziness of the lateral type of child and fatigue and irritability in the linear type.
8. Willing to work hard at acquiring physical skills, and emphasis is on excellence of performance of physical feats.
9. Boys are more active and rough in games than girls.
10. Eye-hand coordination is well developed.
11. Bodily growth is more rapid than heart growth, and lungs are not fully developed.
12. Boys develop greater power in shoulder girdle muscles.

Twelve-Year-Old Children

1. Boys' height, 55 to 61 inches; weight 70 to 101 pounds; girls' height, 56 to 62 inches; weight 72 to 107 pounds.

2. Becoming more skillful in the use of small muscles.
3. May be relatively little body change in some cases.
4. Ten hours of sleep is considered average.
5. Heart rate at rest is between 80 and 90.

It is perhaps appropriate to comment on the ranges of height and weight given here. These heights and weights are what might be called a range within a range, and are computed means or averages within larger ranges. In other words, some children at a given age level could possibly weigh much more or less and be much taller or shorter than the ranges indicate. To illustrate how wide a range can be, one study of a large number of children showed that eleven-year-old girls ranged in weight from 45 to 180 pounds.

In those sports organizations where a concentrated effort is being made to conduct programs to meet the physical needs of all children, there is a strong likelihood that desirable contributions are being made to physical development. On the contrary, some sports programs as now operated cannot be justified of their contribution to physical development of all children.

GUIDELINES FOR PHYSICAL DEVELOPMENT THROUGH CHILDREN'S SPORTS

It is important to set forth some guidelines for physical development if we are to meet with any degree of success in our attempts to provide for physical development of children through sports. The reason for this is to assure, at least to some extent, that our efforts in attaining optimum physical development through sports will be based upon a scientific approach. These guidelines might well take the form of valid *concepts of physical development.* This approach enables us to give serious consideration to what is known about how children grow and develop. Thus, we can select sports experiences that are compatible with the physical developmental process. The following list of concepts of physical development are accompanied by certain implications for children's sports.

1. **Physical Development and Change Is Continuous, Orderly, Progressive, and Differentiated.** In the early years, sports programs, if considered at all, might well be characterized by large muscle activities. As the child develops, more difficult types of skills and activities can be introduced so that sports experiences progress in a way that is compatible with the

child's development. For young children, adults should give serious consideration to what I have identified as "Preparatory Games" in Chapters 9–11. These activities can serve as "lead ups" to more complex games that require more refinement of skills.

2. **Physical Development Is Controlled by Both Heredity and Environment.** The sports program should be planned in such a way to contribute to the innate capacities of each child. Attempts should be made to establish an environmental climate where all children have an equal opportunity for wholesome participation. Some organizations and leagues require that every child be allowed to participate at least some of the time. This means that no one child will spend all of his or her time "warming the bench." Also some games can be modified to meet the needs of all children. In this regard, the following study by Martens et al.[1] is of interest. They found that younger children often have problems playing baseball using adult rules because pitchers lack ability to throw consistently and batters have trouble hitting erratically thrown balls. A modification of adult rules allowed the team coach to pitch to batters. More offensive and defensive activity occurred in the nontraditional games than in traditional and older league games.

3. **Differences in Physical Development Occur at Each Age Level.** This implies that there should be a wide variety of activities to meet the needs of children at various developmental levels. Most of the children whom I surveyed played three sports and sometimes more. While gearing sports activities to meet the needs of a particular group of children, attempts should also be made to provide for individual differences of children within the group. As mentioned in Chapter 1, it is extremely important to classify children's sports teams for competition on the basis of physical fitness, skill level and biological age—not on chronological age only. Also participants should be encouraged to participate in different sports and experience different positions within a given sports activity.

4. **Needs of a Physical Nature Must Be Satisfied if a Child Is to Function Effectively.** Sports experiences should be planned to provide an adequate activity yield. (Physical activity yield will be discussed in detail later in the chapter.) Sports activities should be vigorous enough to meet the physical needs of children and, at the same time, motivating enough so

---

[1]Martens, Rainer et al, A Field Study of Traditional and Nontraditional Children's Baseball, *Research Quarterly for Exercise and Sports,* December 1984.

that they will desire to perpetuate the sports experience at home and in their own neighborhood.

5. **Various Parts of the Body Develop at Different Rates and at Different Ages.** Undue strain to the point of excessive fatigue should be avoided in sports activities. Coaches and parents should be aware of fatigue symptoms so that children are not likely to go beyond their physical capacity. Perhaps the use of large muscles should predominate sports activities, at least for children in the 6–8-year-old range.

6. **The Individual's Own Growth Pattern Will Vary From That of Others Both as to Time and Rate.** It might be well to compare a child's performance with his or her own previous achievements rather than that of classmates. It should be recognized that we should not expect the same standards of performance from all children in any given activity due to individual differences. This is one of the important features of activities such as gymnastics which allows the child to compete against himself or herself as well as against natural forces.

7. **There Are Early Maturers and Late Maturers.** This concept suggests the importance of proper grouping of children within given sports activities. The coach and parent should be aware as to when it is most profitable to classify children either homogeneously or heterogeneously for certain kinds of sports experiences. The same things applies here as in concept number 3.

8. **The Level of Physical Maturation of the Child Often Has a Significant Effect on Learning.** Children should not be expected to achieve beyond their ability levels. A critical examination of the physical needs of children listed previously should be useful in applying this concept.

9. **Physical Differences May Have a Marked Effect on Personality.** A variety of sports experiences should be provided in an effort to give each child a chance to find some successful achievement within his or her own physical capacity. The coach should set the example for children to learn to be respectful of physical differences by helping children to use their particular body type in the most advantageous way.

Experience has shown that when sports programs for children are planned and implemented on the basis of what is known about how they grow and develop, there is a greater likelihood that worthwhile contributions can be made to physical development. Adherence to valid concepts of physical development is considered one of the best ways of accomplishing this goal.

EVALUATING CONTRIBUTIONS OF
SPORTS TO PHYSICAL DEVELOPMENT

Some attempt should be made to assess the potential contribution made by those sports experiences that we provide for children. One of the first steps in this direction is to consider the physical objectives, or what we are trying to do for children physically. The broad physical objectives of children's sports suggested in Chapter 2 consisted of (1) maintaining a suitable level of physical fitness, and (2) developing skill and ability.

In determining whether or not sports experiences are contributing to the child's physical fitness, consideration needs to be given to the identification of specific components comprising the broad aspect of physical fitness. As mentioned previously, there is not complete agreement with the identification of the components of physical fitness. However, the following information provided by the President's Council on Physical Fitness and Sports considers certain components to be basic as follows.

1. **Muscular Strength.** This refers to the contraction power of the muscles. The strength of muscles is usually measured by dynamometers or tensiometers, which record the amount of force particular muscle groups can apply in a single maximum effort. Our existence and effectiveness depend upon our muscles. All movements of the body or any of its parts are impossible without action by muscles attached to the skeleton. Muscles perform vital functions of the body as well. The heart is a muscle; death occurs when it ceases to contract. Breathing, digestion, and elimination are impossible without muscular contractions. These vital muscular functions are influenced by exercising the skeletal muscles; the heart beats faster, the blood circulates through the body at a greater rate, breathing comes deep and rapid, and perspiration breaks out on the surface of the skin.

2. **Muscular Endurance.** Muscular endurance is the ability of the muscles to perform work. Two variations of muscular endurance are recognized: *isometric,* whereby a maximum static muscular contraction is held; *isotonic,* whereby the muscles continue to raise and lower a submaximal load, as in weight training or performing push-ups. In the isometric form, the muscles maintain a fixed length; in the isotonic form, they alternately shorten and lengthen. Muscular endurance must assume some muscle strength, however, there are distinctions between the two;

muscle groups of the same strength may possess different degrees of endurance.

3. **Circulatory-Respiratory Endurance.** Circulatory-respiratory endurance is characterized by moderate contractions of large muscle groups for relatively long periods of time during which maximal adjustments of the circulatory-respiratory system to the activity are necessary, as in distance running or swimming. Obviously, strong and enduring muscles are needed. However, by themselves, they are not enough; they do not guarantee well-developed circulatory and respiratory functions.

In **addition to the basic three above, other components of physical fitness to be considered are:**

1. *Muscular Power:* ability to release maximum muscular force in the shortest time. Example—standing long jump.
2. *Agility:* speed in changing direction, or body positions. Example—dodging run.
3. *Speed:* rapidity with which successive movements of the same kind are performed. Example—50-yard dash.
4. *Flexibility:* range of movements in a joint or a sequence of joints. Example—touch fingers to floor without bending knees.
5. *Balance:* ability to maintain position and equilibrium both in movement (dynamic balance) and while stationary (static balance). Example—walking on a line or balance beam (dynamic); standing on one foot (static).
6. *Coordination:* working together of the muscles and organs of the human body in the performance of a specific task. Example—throwing or catching an object.

Having an understanding of the above components of physical fitness should be extremely helpful to the coach in his or her efforts to evaluate the extent to which certain sports experiences contribute to the maintenance of a suitable level of physical fitness. In fact, in planning sports experiences for children, certain questions may be raised in connection with the activities used to bring about these experiences.

1. Does the activity provide for contraction power of muscles (muscular strength)?
2. Are there opportunities in the activity for isometric and/or isotonic muscular activity (muscular endurance)?
3. Does the activity provide for moderate contraction of large muscles for specified periods of time (circulatory-respiratory endurance)?

4. Does the activity involve ability to release maximum muscular force in a short period of time (muscular power)?
5. Is there opportunity in the activity to utilize speed in changing direction (agility)?
6. Does the activity require rapidity with successive movements of the same kind (speed)?
7. Does the activity involve various degrees of bending at the joints (flexibility)?
8. Is the activity one that involves the ability to maintain position and equilibrium (balance)?
9. Is the activity concerned with the working together of the muscles and organs in specific task performance (coordination)?

Of course, it is not to be expected that all activities will involve all of the components of physical fitness. For example, while a certain sports activity may require various degrees of agility, it may not necessarily involve a great deal of muscular strength. However, it would be possible to select enough activities with sufficient balance of the components over a period of time so that activities as a group could contribute to the total physical fitness of the child.

It should also be clearly understood that there are limits to which we may wish to conduct activities that involve certain components of physical fitness. For instances, it is not likely that with young children we would want to utilize too many activities involving circulatory-respiratory endurance. (For example, some studies have shown that long distance running by children can adversely affect long bone growth.) This, of course, presupposes that coaches will have a sufficient understanding of the traits and characteristics of children at the various age levels.

Not only should the coach consider this approach in planning and practicing activities, but for purposes of value assessment after activities have been conducted. With this procedure, some judgment could be made with reference to how well a given activity attained a given purpose. It should be kept in mind that the extent to which a sports activity may contribute to any given component of physical fitness will likely be contingent upon a variety of factors. Included among such factors are the ability level of a given group of children; number of children on a team; general nature of the activity; difficulty in providing for individual differences where the activity takes place; and above all, the coach's input and behavior.

It should be obvious that any assessment made in connection with this approach is limited because of subjectivity. Nevertheless, coaches' judgments in such matters should contain a great deal of validity, provided, as mentioned previously, that they have a clear understanding of the growing organism and the traits and characteristics at the various age levels. A rating scale that I have prepared and used with success for making such judgments is shown in Figure 3 and may be used as follows: The sports activities are listed under the heading ACTIVITIES. The coach then poses the question to himself or herself, "What is the value of this activity in terms of its contribution to the various components of physical fitness?" Using the rating scale, judgments are made accordingly. Adding the horizontal totals and dividing by nine will indicate an overall average for an activity. Adding the vertical totals and dividing by the number of activities will give the average value of each of the components of all of the activities.

The second aspect of physical development through sports—development of skill and ability—could be evaluated in this same general manner; that is, a similar type rating scale could be used to assess the extent to which a sports activity requires the use of certain skills. Figure 4 depicts a rating scale for this purpose. (Chapter 7 will explain in detail how to perform these various skills.)

PHYSICAL ACTIVITY YIELD

Another approach in determining the extent to which children's sports contribute to physical fitness is one that I have identified as *physical activity yield.* This is concerned with the amount of time that a majority of the children are meaningfully active in a given sports experience. The term *majority* can have a range of from one more than half to all of the children on a team. Generally, the majority of children is considered to be 80 percent of them. This would mean that there would be activity yield for a team if four out of five children were meaningfully active at one time. Meaningfully active is interpreted as the children being involved in a sports activity that has a specific purpose and objective.

Reflecting back to my own personal experience with physical activity yield as a child in the early 1920s, I was a centerfielder on a Class F sandlot baseball team in a large metropolitan area in the midwest. I had very little action in this position probably because most of the opposing batters could not hit the ball that far. Thus, I stood there practically

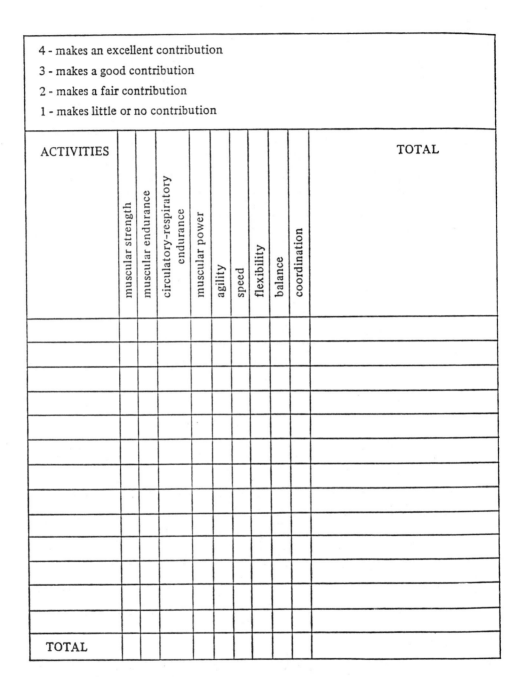

| 4 - makes an excellent contribution |
| 3 - makes a good contribution |
| 2 - makes a fair contribution |
| 1 - makes little or no contribution |

ACTIVITIES	muscular strength	muscular endurance	circulatory-respiratory endurance	muscular power	agility	speed	flexibility	balance	coordination	TOTAL
TOTAL										

Figure 3. Scale for Rating Potential Contributions of Sports to Physical Fitness

4 - provides an excellent opportunity

3 - provides a good opportunity

2 - provides a fair opportunity

1 - provides little or no opportunity

ACTIVITIES	LOCOMOTOR								AUXILIARY						PROPULSION RETRIEVAL				TOTAL
	walking	running	leaping	jumping	hopping	galloping	skipping	sliding	starting	stopping	dodging	pivoting	landing	falling	throwing	striking	kicking	catching	
TOTAL																			

Figure 4. Scale for Rating Opportunities for Practice of Skills

motionless for most of the game. Later, as a high school basketball player, I experienced a great deal of physical activity yield because I seemed to be running up and down the floor "forever." Many years later these experiences may no doubt have been what caused me to characterize the game of baseball in the following manner: Two people playing catch (pitcher and catcher) while a third person (batter) tries to prevent it. Seven others (basemen and fielders) standing and watching, and still eight others (opposing team) are sitting and watching.

It should be interesting to note that while the game of baseball tends to provide a relatively small amount of activity yield as described above, it nevertheless is a very popular activity—our national passtime, no less. Moreover, it was the third most popular sport among the children in my surveys.

The physical activity yield approach differs appreciably from the previously mentioned approach in that it is not as precise and definitive; that is, it provides only for a recognition of general physical activity engaged in by children and not for specific physical fitness components. Neither does it provide for consideration of skills used in the various activities.

In any event, the important factor to consider is that some attempt be made to arrive at an evaluation of the extent to which sports activities contribute to the physical development of children. This, of course, requires that each sports activity be carefully analyzed for its possible potential contribution to physical development, along with how the activity should be conducted, so that the most desirable and worthwhile results will be obtained.

Chapter 4

SOCIAL DEVELOPMENT OF CHILDREN THROUGH SPORTS

Sports enthusiasts have been somewhat generous in praising this experience as an outstanding medium for contributing to social development of children. This was shown in a recent analysis that I made of over 50 books that dealt in some way with children's physical activity programs, including sports.

The purpose of this analysis was to identify declarative statements that proclaimed positive contributions to the various forms of development—physical, social, emotional, and intellectual. Forty-five percent of the total number of statements indicated contributions to social development, followed by physical development with 29 percent, emotional development with 17 percent, and intellectual development with 9 percent.

While the above attests to the subjective pronouncements of the social values of children's physical activity programs and sports, at the same time it is interesting to note that little research has been conducted to build an objective foundation under this long-held theoretical postulation. In order to examine this more thoroughly, I made a documentary analysis of children's physical activity programs and sports research reported in the *Research Quarterly of Exercise and Sports* over a 20-year period (80 issues). Seven percent of all the studies reported met the criteria that was established to determine if a study was concerned with children in the 6–12 year age range. Sixty-seven percent of this number dealt with whole or part of the physical aspect. This compared with 12 percent with the emotional aspect, 11 percent with the intellectual aspect, and 10 percent with the social aspect. Moreover, in a very small percentage of the cases it was demonstrated that physical activity and sports programs made significant contributions to social development.

Most of the research that has been done in this general area has been devoted to relationships between social and physical factors. The majority of these findings generally show that the most popular children are those who are most adept in the performance of physical skills required in sports. In this regard, it is interesting to note that some studies of boys and girls reveal that both sexes express a preference for good school marks over excelling in sports and being popular. It has also been reported that many children selected as outstanding academically or athletically were listed as popular more often than children not in these categories. When outstanding students, athletes, and student-athletes (outstanding academically *and* athletically) are compared as to popularity, it is generally found that among boys, athletes were somewhat more popular, while among girls, student-athletes seemed to be slightly more popular.

It is interesting to note that some recent studies have yielded slightly different results. For example, in studying the role of sports as a social status determinant for children, Chase and Dummer[1] had a total of 227 boys and 251 girls in Grades 4, 5, and 6 complete a questionnaire to determine which criteria were most important in determining personal, female, and male popularity. Personal popularity was answered by the girls and boys according to "what would make you well liked by your classmates." Female and male popularity was determined by asking both boys and girls to decide "what would make (girls, for female subjects, and boys, for male subjects) well liked by your classmates." For boys, it was revealed that sports have become more important and academic achievement less important in determining personal popularity. Boys reported sports to be the most important determinant of personal and male popularity and appearance as the most important determinant of female popularity. Sports and appearance became more important for boys with each higher grade level. Girls reported appearance to be the most important determinant of personal, male, and female popularity. For girls, appearance became more important with each higher grade level.

Admittedly, the whole area of sociality and children's sports is difficult to study objectively, and this may be a part of the reason why so little research has been undertaken.

The above should not be interpreted to mean that sports experiences have little to contribute to social development of children. On the contrary, the *potential* values of sports in making positive contributions to social

---

[1]Chase, Melissa A. and Dummer, Gail M., The Role of Sports as a Social Determinant for Children, *Research Quarterly for Exercise and Sports,* December 1992.

development are tremendous. One of the major functions of this chapter is to explore some of the ways in which this might be accomplished.

SOCIAL NEEDS OF CHILDREN

In Chapter 3 it was mentioned that it is a relatively easy matter to identify specific components of physical fitness, but this does not neccessarily hold true for components of social fitness. Thus, in the absence of definitive components of social fitness, other directions need to be pursued in our efforts to help children achieve satisfactory levels of social fitness.

Social maturity and, hence, social fitness may be expressed in terms of fulfillment of certain social needs. In other words, if certain social needs are being adequately met, the child should be in a better position to realize social fitness and achieve social development. Among the general needs we should give consideration to are (1) *the need for affection,* which involves acceptance and approval of persons, (2) *the need for belonging* which involves acceptance and approval of the group, and (3) *the need for mutuality,* which involves cooperation, mutual helpfulness, and group loyalty. The conditions for meeting these needs are inherent in many sports experiences.

In addition to these general needs, specific needs are reflected in the developmental characteristics of growing children. Many such characteristics are identified in the following lists at the different age levels.

Five-Year-Old Children

1. Interested in neighborhood games that involve any number of children.
2. Plays various games to test his skill.
3. Enjoys other children and like to be with them.
4. Interests are largely self-centered.
5. Seems to get along best in small groups.
6. Shows an interest in home activities.
7. Imitates when he plays.
8. Gets along well in taking turns.
9. Respects the belongings of other people.

Six-Year-Old Children

1. Self-centered and has need for praise.
2. Likes to be first.
3. Indifferent to sex distinction.
4. Enjoys group play when groups tend to be small.
5. Likes parties but behavior may not always be decorous.
6. The majority enjoy school association and have a desire to learn.
7. Interests in conduct of friends.
8. Boys like to fight and wrestle with peers to prove masculinity.
9. Shows an interest in group approval.

Seven-Year-Old Children

1. Wants recognition for individual achievements.
2. Sex differences are not of great importance.
3. Not always a good loser.
4. Conversation often centers around family.
5. Learning to stand up for own rights.
6. Interested in friends and is not influenced by their social or economic status.
7. May have nervous habits such as nail biting, tongue sucking, scratching, or pulling at ear.
8. Attaining orientation in time.
9. Gets greater enjoyment from group play.
10. Shows greater signs of cooperative efforts.

Eight-Year-Old Children

1. Girls are careful of their clothes, but boys are not.
2. Leaves many things uncompleted.
3. Has special friends.
4. Has longer periods of peaceful play.
5. Does not like playing alone.
6. Enjoys dramatizing.
7. Starts collections.
8. Enjoys school and dislikes staying home.
9. Likes variety.
10. Recognition of property rights is well established.
11. Responds well to group activity.

12. Interest will focus on friends of own sex.
13. Beginning of the desire to become a member of a club.

Nine-Year-Old Children

1. Wants to be like others, talk like others, and look like them.
2. Girls are becoming more interested in their clothes.
3. Is generally a conformist and may be afraid of that which is different.
4. Able to be on his own.
5. Able to be fairly responsible and dependable.
6. Some firm and loyal friendships may develop.
7. Increasing development of qualities of leadership and followership.
8. Increasing interest in activities involving challenges and adventure.
9. Increasing participation in varied and organized group activities.

Ten-Year-Old Children

1. Begins to recognize the fallibility of adults.
2. Moving more into a peer-centered society.
3. Both boys and girls are amazingly self-dependent.
4. Self-reliance has grown and at the same time intensified groups feelings are required.
5. Divergence between the two sexes is widening.
6. Great team loyalties are developing.
7. Beginning to identify with one's social contemporaries of the same sex.
8. Relatively easy to appeal to his reason.
9. On the whole, he has a fairly critical sense of justice.
10. Boys show their friendship with other boys by wrestling and jostling with each other, while girls walk around with arms around each other as friends.
11. Interest in people, in the community, and affairs of the world is keen.
12. Interested in social problems in an elementary way and likes to take part in discussions.

Eleven-Year-Old Children

1. Internal guiding standards have been set up, and although guided by what is done by other children, he will modify his behavior in line with those standards already set up.

2. Does a number of socially acceptable things, not because they are right or wrong.
3. Although obsessed by standards of peers, he is anxious for social approval of adults.
4. Need for social companionship of children their own age.
5. Liking for organized games becoming more prominent.
6. Girls are likely to be self-conscious in the presence of boys and are usually much more mature than boys.
7. Team spirit is very strong.
8. Boys' and girls' interests are not always the same, and there may be some antagonism between the sexes.
9. Often engages in silly behavior, such as giggling and clowning.
10. Girls are more interested in social appearance than are boys.

Twelve-Year-Old Children

1. Increasing identification of self with other children of own sex.
2. Increasing recognition of fallibility of adults.
3. May see himself as a child and adults as adults.
4. Getting ready to make the difficult transition to adolescence.
5. Pressure is being placed on individual at this level to begin to assume adult responsibilities.

It should be obvious that the above social characteristics of different age children should be taken into account if we are to meet with any degree of success in our efforts in the direction of social development through sports.

GUIDELINES FOR SOCIAL DEVELOPMENT THROUGH SPORTS

Guidelines for social development are set forth here in the same manner that guidelines for physical development through sports were proposed in the previous chapter; that is, these guidelines take the form of valid *concepts of social development.* When we have some basis for social behavior of children as they grow and develop we are then in a better position to select and conduct sports activities that are likely to be compatible with social development. The following list of concepts of social development with implications for children's sports are submitted with this general idea in mind.

1. **Interpersonal Relationships Are Based on Social Needs.** All children should be given an equal opportunity in sports participation. Moreover, the coach should impress upon children their importance to the team. This can be done in connection with the team or group effort, which is so essential to successful participation. It is encouraging that some baseball leagues have a rule that every child must play and that every player must play in the infield at least part of the time.

2. **A Child Can Develop His or Her Self-Concept Through Undertaking Roles.** A child is more likely to be aware of his or her particular abilities if given the opportunity to play different positions on a team. Rotation of such responsibilities as team captains tends to provide opportunity for self-expression of children through role playing.

3. **There Are Various Degrees of Interaction Between Individuals and Groups.** The sports experience should provide an outstanding setting for the child to develop interpersonal interaction. The coach has the opportunity to observe children in action rather than in only sedentary situations. Consequently, the coach is in a good position to guide integrative experiences by helping children to see the importance of satisfactory interrelationships in sports group situations.

4. **Choosing and Being Chosen—An Expression of a Basic Need—is a Foundation of Interpersonal Relationships.** As often as possible, children should be given the opportunity for choosing teammates, partners and the like. However, great caution should be taken by the coach to see that this is carried out in an equitable way. At practice sessions the coach should devise ways of choice so that certain children are not always selected last or left out entirely.

5. **Language Is a Basic Means and Essential Accompaniment of Socialization.** Children can be taught the language of the body through using the names of its parts as they participate in sports. For example, "Good arm, Jane," or "Put some foot into it Joe." This is an important dimension in the development of body awareness. (This will be discussed in greater detail in Chapter 6.) Sports experiences should be such that there is opportunity for oral expression among and between children. For example, in the *evaluation phase* of a sports learning situation, children have a fine opportunity for meaningful expression if the evaluation is skillfully guided by the coach. (This aspect of teaching and learning will be discussed at length in Chapter 8.)

6. **Learning to Play Roles Is a Process of Social Development.** A child may be given the opportunity to play as many roles as possible in the sports experience. This could be involved in the organization and administration of sports activities such as selection of activities, making rules of play, and helping others with skills. Doing a physical skill is in itself the playing of a role, such as being a better thrower, catcher, and the like. Thus, the very medium of sports activities is the process of social adjustment.

7. **Integrative Interaction Tends to Promote Social Development.** The key word in this process to promote social development is *action,* which is the basis for sports participation. Sports participation is unique in its potential to accomplish integrative interaction, and thus promote social development. Spontaneity can be considered as one of the desired outcomes of integrative experiences, which means the opportunity for actions and feelings expressed by the child as he or she really is. Active play is perhaps the most important aspect of life for children, and thus, spontaneous actions and feelings are best expressed through physical activity.

8. **Resistance to Domination Is an Active Attempt to Maintain One's Integrity.** The coach might well consider child resistance as a possible indicator of coach domination. If this occurs, the coach might look into his or her actions, which may be dominating the sports teaching-learning situation. Child resistance should be interpreted as a sign of a healthful personality, and a wise coach will likely be able to direct the energy into constructive channels to promote social development. A very natural outlet for this frustrated energy is found in desirable activities presented in a sports program.

9. **Interpersonal Interaction Between Children Is a Basis for Choice.** If children are left out by other children, this symptom should be studied with care to see if this is an indication of poor interpersonal relationships with other children. Very interesting aspects of interpersonal relationships can be observed by the wise coach. Children may realize the value of a child to a specific activity and accept such a child accordingly. On the other hand, they may be likely to accept their friends regardless of ability in sports skills.

10. **A Child, in and as a Result of Belonging to a Group, Develops Differently Than He or She Can as an Individual Alone.** Most sports activities provide for an outstanding opportunity for children to engage actively in group experiences. Merely being a member of a team can be a most rewarding experience for a child. If properly conducted, sports

activities should provide an optimal situation for desirable social development because children focus their greatest personal interest in active play.

SOME POSSIBILITIES FOR
SOCIAL DEVELOPMENT THROUGH SPORTS

It has already been suggested that the sports "laboratory" should present near-ideal surroundings and environment for the social development of children. It has also been indicated that coaches are convinced that this area provides some of the best means for teaching vital social skills. The following generalized discussion is intended to elaborate some of these possibilities.

There are numerous sports situations through which children may gain a better understanding of the importance of cooperation. By their very nature, many games depend upon the cooperation of group members in achieving a common goal. In skills such as throwing and catching there must be a coordinated action of the thrower and catcher. In certain kinds of gymnastic activities, children participate and learn together in groups of three—two children assisting the performer and the others taking turns in performing. In these and countless other situations the importance of cooperating together for the benefit of the individual and the group is readily discerned.

In this general regard, the following study by Berlage[2] is of interest. The researcher studied the similarities between children's competitive team sports and the typical corporate or business environment. Two research questions were posed: (1) Does the structural organization of children's soccer and ice hockey organizations resemble that of American corporations? and (2) Are the values of children's competitive sports similar to corporate values? Questionnaires were distributed to 222 Connecticut and New York fathers of 11- or 12-year-old sons on soccer and ice hockey teams. Through observations and interviews, it was found that the structural organization of the children's ice hockey and soccer programs clearly resembled that of corporations. An organizational chart illustrated the hierarchies and divisions in a youth soccer program, and it was also found that the values stressed in competitive sports are similar

---

[2]Berlage, G., Are Children's Competitive Team Sports Socializing Agents for Corporate America, Paper presented at the North American Society for the Sociology of Sport, Fort Worth, TX, November 12–15, 1981.

to corporate values. The fathers selected teamwork (cooperation) as the most important sports attribute that would contribute to success in business. The importance of learning to be part of a team was a constant theme in the fathers' responses. Although some fathers expressed misgivings about the amount of politics in the team selection process and the inconveniences of complying with practice and travel schedules, most fathers had positive attitudes toward competitive youth sports. It was concluded that those who have participated in competitive sports have an advantage over others who are not socialized in these values, skills, and attitudes.

Issues that come up as a result of certain misunderstandings in sports activities give rise to the exercise of wholesome social controls. The relationships of these controls in sports experiences to those in community living might possibly be understood in varying degrees by children at the different age levels. In these situations, outstanding settings are provided for the development of problem-solving techniques in which children are placed to make value judgments.

Some coaches have observed that while sports provide opportunities to encourage interpersonal communication and understanding among children, at the same time these opportunities are occasionally manifested in the form of minor conflicts. A procedure used to help solve such minor conflicts has been suggested by Robert Horrocks. He refers to it as the "talking bench" where two children sit until they have agreed upon the origin of their conflict and resolved it to the satisfaction of both.

The above discussion included but a few of the numerous possibilities for social control, social interaction, and thus social development, which are likely to be inherent in the sports experience. Admittedly, this does not accrue automatically, and any degree of success in social development through sports rests heavily upon the coach and parents as well.

IMPLICATIONS OF RESEARCH IN SOCIAL BEHAVIOR OF CHILDREN

As has been mentioned previously, not a great deal of research has been undertaken in the field of sports in relation to social development of children. This being the case, we should consider the psychological research that has been conducted in social development so that we can draw some implications for sports. This is to say that in utilizing such findings, we will be better able to conduct sports experiences that are more likely to result in positive social development. A report by the National Institute of Education provides some information that might be useful.

The purpose of this report was to provide elementary school teachers with a summary of psychological research concerned with the social development of young children. In submitting the report, it was noted that caution should prevail with reference to basic research and practical implications. In this regard, the following suggestions are submitted.

1. What seems "true" at one point in time often becomes "false" when new information becomes available or when new theories change the interpretation of old findings.
2. Substantial problems arise in any attempt to formulate practical suggestions for professionals in one discipline based on research findings from another discipline.
3. Throughout the report, recommendations for teachers have been derived from logical extensions of experimental findings and classroom adaptations of experimental procedures.
4. Some of the proposed procedures may prove unworkable in the classroom, even though they may make sense from a psychological perspective.
5. When evaluating potential applications of psychological findings it is important to remember that psychological research is usually designed to derive probability statements about the behavior of groups of people.
6. Individual teachers (coaches) may work better with a procedure that is, on the average, less effective.

The following list of generalizations, which have been derived from the findings are accompanied by possible general implications for children's sports. In considering these implications, the above cautions should be kept in mind. Moreover, each individual coach or parent will no doubt be able to draw his or her own implications and make practical applications that apply to particular situations.

1. **Reasoning with an Emphasis on Consequences for Other People Is Associated with the Development of a Humanistic Concern for Others.** Coaches might give consideration to encouragement of social behavior in the sports experience by discussing the implications of children's and

coaches' actions for the feelings of others; poor performers should be encouraged rather than ridiculed.

2. **Children Tend to Show Empathy Toward Individuals Similar to Themselves.** In the sports experience it is important to emphasize the likenesses of people; while all children may differ in one or more characteristics they still are more alike than they are different.

3. **Children May Learn Techniques for Positive Social Interaction by Observing Children Who Are Behaving Cooperatively.** In team games, particularly, cooperation of each individual is very important to the success of the team; the coach can suggest ways children can cooperate and reinforce children when these suggestions are followed.

4. **The More Frequently Children Voluntarily Practice Social Skills, the More Likely They Are to Use These Skills in Less Structured Situations.** In the sports situation, children can be assigned certain responsibilities that require the practice of social skills. The coach can coordinate this experience with the parent, and each can determine the results of the other's efforts.

5. **Children Are Likely to Use Behaviors for Which They Have Been Reinforced.** The coach can focus his or her attention on children who are cooperating, sharing, and helping the coach and other children in the sports situation.

6. **Children Are Likely to Imitate Behaviors for Which They See Other Children Being Reinforced.** The coach can compliment those children who are saying cooperative, helpful things to each other, particularly in participation in team games. At the same time, the coach should consider simultaneously ignoring negative social interactions of children.

7. **Children Are Likely to Help and Share When They Have Seen Someone Else Do It, Particularly if They Know and Like the Model.** The coach and parents can take the lead by providing examples of sharing, helping and cooperating.

8. **Ignored Behavior May Increase at First, but Eventually It Is Likely to Decrease if the Child Does not Receive Reinforcement from Other Sources.** The coach may wish to pointedly ignore misbehavior whenever possible by turning away from a misbehaving child and attending to a child who is behaving appropriately. Obviously, all misbehavior cannot be ignored because in some instances such misbehavior might be concerned with safety factors in the sports experience. Thus, it is sometimes appropriate for the coach to act expediently.

9. Consistent, Immediate Punishment May Tend to Discourage the Behavior it Follows. When this is necessary, the coach might consider choosing mild punishment related to the activity, which can follow misbehavior immediately. For example, if a child is misusing a piece of material such as a ball, it can be removed, at least temporarily.

10. **Reasoning Can Increase Children's Awareness of the Needs of Others, and It (Reasoning) Is a Form of Attention That Should Be Limited to Occasions When Children Are Behaving Appropriately.** In many sports teaching-learning situations there is a need for certain rules and regulations. It might be well to discuss the reasoning behind rules when children are following the rules and *not* when the rules are disobeyed. However, this does not necessarily preclude a negative approach if a given situation warrants it.

In closing this discussion, it should be reiterated that each individual reader will no doubt be able to draw his or her own implications and make practical applications that apply to particular sports situations.

EVALUATING CONTRIBUTIONS OF SPORTS TO SOCIAL DEVELOPMENT

It has already been mentioned that coaches place great store in the contributions of sports to social development of children. It has also been suggested that little solid scientific evidence is available to support this belief. This makes it all the more important that coaches and parents as well examine critically those sports experiences that are being provided for children.

Processes for Evaluating Social Growth in Sports

In the past, most of what has been done in this area has been of a subjective nature. The process of "observation" has been considered satisfactory because it has been felt that for the most part we can merely watch children to see the kinds of relationships that exist between them.

In more recent years, I have approached this problem from a more scientific standpoint, using certain *sociometric techniques* with varying degrees of success. Included among such techniques are (1) sociograms, (2) sociographs, and (3) social distance scales.

Sociograms

In this technique, a child is usually asked to name in order of preference those persons liked best on a team. In the sports situation, a child may be asked to name those he or she would like to be with or play with most. After the choices are made, the results are plotted on a sociogram.

If two children choose each other, they are known as "mutual choices of pairs." Those not selected by anyone in the group and who do not choose anyone are called "isolates." "Islands" is the name given to pairs or small groups of mutual choices not selected by any in the large group. While the sociogram is a worthwhile device for identifying certain aspects of interpersonal relationships, it is a time-consuming procedure and for this reason is not one of the more popular methods used.

Sociographs

The sociograph is a more expedient and practical way of tabulating and interpreting data. Instead of plotting as in a sociogram, choices are recorded in tabular form opposite the names of children. This readily shows the number of rejections, mutual choices, choices received, and choices given.

Social Distance Scales

This sociometric technique has been used in research in social psychology for over fifty years. In this procedure, each member of a group is asked to check the other members according to certain degrees of social intimacy such as:

1. Would like to have him as one of my friends.
2. Would like to have him on my team, but not as a close friend.
3. Would like to be with him once in a while, but not often or for very long.
4. Do not mind his being on the team, but I do not want anything to do with him.
5. Wish he were not on the team.

This procedure can be used as a sports experience social distance scale to attempt to determine the general social tone of a team. Team social distance scores on each individual child can be obtained by arbitrarily weighting the items listed above. For example, if a child was checked two times for item number one ($2 \times 1 = 2$); six times for item two ($6 \times 2 = 12$); eight times for item three ($8 \times 3 = 24$); three times for item four ($3 \times$

4 = 12); and one time for item five (1 × 5 = 5) the total score would be 55. (The lower the score the greater the acceptance by the group and the less the social distance.)

These data can be used to determine, with some degree of objectivity, the extent to which the sports experience has contributed to social relationships; that is, a coach can compare scores before and after a group of children have been involved in a particular sports experience. This can be done on an individual game basis when a team has won or when it has lost. Also, it can be done at the beginning and at the end of an entire season to measure whatever social growth may have taken place among the participants.

Over a period of years, I have used all of the above sociometric techniques when I have been asked to make an assessment of a certain children's sports program. In some instances, the results have provided guidance in efforts to obtain a better understanding of social relationships and thus contribute to social development. It is recognized that most all coaches are aware of those obvious factors concerned with group social structure. However, the many aspects of interpersonal relationships that are not so obvious can be difficult to discern. It is the purpose of sociometric techniques to assist in the emergence of these relationships.

Any discussion about social development and sports would not be complete without some mention of *sportsmanship.* Thus, I would like to close this chapter with some general comments on this subject.

Sportsmanship is concerned with the social conduct of a participant who is thought of as a good loser and a gracious winner. It seems that in recent years certain behavior of participants and audiences as well, have put a serious strain on what has been considered to be good sportsmanship. Not only has *antisportsmanship* been evident at the higher levels of sports participation, but it has seeped down into children's sports as well.

This condition prompted the National Youth Sports Coaches Association to conduct a summit on the subject in San Antonio, Texas in August 1992. At this meeting Bob Bierscheid,[3] Chairman of the NYCSA National Board of Directors, commented that, "Our purpose for sponsoring this national summit was to help further define the National Standards for Youth Sports for youth leagues across America." And further, "Our mission is to encourage every league to implement these standards.

---

[3]Donegan, Craig. Sportsmanship Takes a Dive in America, *Youth Sport Coach,* Winter 1992.

Then and only then will we have begun to bring the proper focus on sportsmanship that is needed in youth sports."

To promote these aims, the NYSCA has produced the codes of ethics for coaches and parents that I cited in Chapter 1. Also, the Association has installed grievance procedures through which coaches may be decertified for behavior at odds with the Association Standards.

Participants at the NYSCA sportsmanship summit agreed that children enjoy sports most when they are taught and encouraged to sharpen their playing skills in an atmosphere of sportsmanship and fair play. My own studies tend to agree with this type of thinking.

Chapter 5

EMOTIONAL DEVELOPMENT OF CHILDREN THROUGH SPORTS

In the brief discussion of emotion in Chapter 2 it was suggested that the emotional objective of sports should imply that sympathetic guidance should be provided in meeting anxieties, joys, and sorrows and help given in developing aspirations and security. In order to attempt to reach this objective, we might well consider emotions from a standpoint of the growing child in terms of maturing emotionally.

For purposes of this discussion, I will consider *maturity* as being concerned with a state of readiness on the part of the organism. The term is most frequently used in connection with age relationships. For example, it may be said that "Johnny is mature for six years of age." Simply stated, emotional maturity is the process of acting one's age.

Generally speaking, emotional maturity will be achieved through a gradual accumulation of mild and pleasant emotions. On the contrary, emotional immaturity indicates that unpleasant emotions have accumulated too rapidly for the individual to absorb. In order to pursue a sensible course in helping the child become more emotionally mature, there are certain factors concerned with emotional development that need to be taken into account. Some of these factors are the subject of the ensuing discussion.

FACTORS CONCERNING EMOTIONAL DEVELOPMENT

Some of the factors concerned with emotional development that need to be considered are: (1) characteristics of childhood emotionality, (2) emotional arousals and reactions, and (3) factors that influence emotionality.

65

Characteristics of Childhood Emotionality

1. **Ordinarily, the Emotions of Children Are not Long Lasting.** A child's emotions may last for a few minutes or less and then terminate rather abruptly. The child gets it "out of his or her system" so-to-speak by expressing it outwardly. In contrast, some adult emotions may be long and drawn out. As children get older, expressing the emotions by overt action is encumbered by certain social restraints. This is to say that what might be socially acceptable at one age level is not necessarily so at another. This may be a reason for some children developing moods, which in a sense are states of emotion drawn out over a period of time and expressed slowly. Typical moods of childhood may be that of "sulking" due to restraint of anger, being "jumpy" from repressed fear, and becoming "humorous" from controlled joy or happiness.

2. **The Emotions of Children Are Likely To Be Intense.** This might be confusing to some adults who do not understand child behavior; that is, they may not be able to see why a child would react rather violently to a situation that to them might appear insignificant.

3. **The Emotions of Children Are Subject to Rapid Change.** A child is capable of shifting rapidly from laughing to crying, or from anger to joy. Although the reason for this is not definitely known, it might be that there is not as much depth of feeling among children as there is among adults. In addition, it could be due to the lack of experience that children have had as well as their state of intellectual development. We do know that young children have a short attention span, which could cause them to change rapidly from one kind of emotion to another.

4. **The Emotions of Children Can Appear with a High Degree of Frequency.** As children get older, they manage to develop the ability to adjust to situations that previously would have caused an emotional reaction. This is probably due to the child's acquiring more experience with various kinds of emotional situations. Perhaps a child learns through experience what is socially acceptable and what is socially unacceptable. This is particularly true if the child is reprimanded in some way following a violent emotional reaction. For this reason, the child may try to confront situations in ways that do not involve an emotional response.

5. **Children Differ in Their Emotional Responses.** One child confronted with a situation that instills fear may run away from the immediate environment. Another might just stand there and cry. Different reactions of children to emotional situations are probably due to a host of

factors. Included among these may be past experiences with a certain kind of emotional situation; willingness of parents and other adults to help children become independent; and family relationships in general.

6. **Strength of Children's Emotions Are Subject to Change.** At some age levels certain kinds of emotions may be weak and later become stronger. Conversely, with some children, emotions that were strong may tend to decline. For example, small children may be timid among strangers, but later when they see there is nothing to fear, the timidity is likely to wane.

Emotional Arousals and Reactions

If we are to understand the emotions of children, we need to take into account those factors of emotional arousal and how children might be expected to react to them. Many different kinds of emotional patterns have been identified. For purposes here, I have arbitrarily selected for discussion the emotional states of fear, worry, anger, jealousy, and joy.

1. **Fear.** It is possible that it is not necessarily the arousal itself, but rather the way something is presented that determines whether there will be a fear reaction. For example, in a practice session if there is a discussion of a certain gymnastic activity in terms of "If you do it that way you will break your neck," it is possible that a fear response will occur. This is one of the many reasons for using a positive approach, especially in the area of sports activities.

A child may react to fear by withdrawing. With very young children this may be in the form of crying or breath holding. With a child under three, and in some older children as well, the "ostrich" approach may be used; that is, he may hide his face in order to get away from it. As children get older, these forms of reaction may decrease or cease altogether because of social pressures. For instance, it may be considered "sissy" to cry, especially among boys. (The validity of this kind of thinking is, of course, open to question.)

In my studies the three greatest fears children have about sports are (1) getting hurt, (2) losing, and (3) not playing well.

2. **Worry.** This might be considered an imaginary form of fear, and it can be a fear not aroused directly from the child's environment. Worry can be aroused by imagining a situation that could possibly arise; that is, a child could worry about not being able to perform well in a certain sports situation. Since worries are likely to be caused by imaginary rather than real conditions, they are not likely to be found in abundance

among very young children. Perhaps the reason for this is that they have not reached a stage of intellectual development where they might imagine certain things that could cause worry. While children will respond to worry in different ways, certain manifestations such as nail biting may be symptomatic of this condition.

3. **Anger.** This emotional response tends to occur more frequently than that of fear. This is probably due to the fact that there are more conditions that incite anger. In addition, some children quickly learn that anger may get attention that otherwise would not be forthcoming. It is likely that as children get older they may show more anger responses than fear responses because they soon see that there is not too much to fear.

Anger is caused by many factors, one of which is interference with movements the child wants to execute. This interference can come from others or by the child's own limitations in ability and physical development. This, of course, can be an important factor in the performance of certain tasks in sports.

Because of individual differences in children, there is a wide variation in anger responses. In general, these responses are either *impulsive* or *inhibited.* In impulsive responses, the child manifests an overt action either toward another person or an object that caused the anger. For instance, a child who collides with a door might take out the anger by hitting or kicking the door. (This form of child behavior is also sometimes manifested by some "adults.") Inhibited responses are likely to be kept under control, and as children mature emotionally they acquire more ability to control their anger.

My studies show that the three greatest causes of anger among children when they participate in sports are: (1) when some players cheat, (2) when someone plays dirty, and (3) getting yelled at.

4. **Jealousy.** This response usually occurs when a child feels a threat of loss of affection. Many psychologists believe that jealousy is closely related to anger. Because of this the child may build up resentment against another person. Jealousy can be very devastating in childhood, and every effort should be made to avoid it.

Jealousy is concerned with social interaction that involves persons the child likes. These individuals can be parents, siblings, teachers, coaches, and peers. There are various ways in which the child may respond. These include (1) being aggressive toward the one he is jealous of, or possibly toward others as well, (2) withdrawing from the person whose affections he thinks have been lost, and (3) possible development of an "I don't care" attitude.

In some cases children will not respond in any of the above ways. They might try to excell over the person of whom they are jealous. In other words, they may tend to do things to impress the person whose affections they thought have been lost.

5. **Joy.** This pleasant emotion is one that we strive for because it is so important in maintaining emotional stability. Causes of joy differ from one age level to another and from one child to another at the same age level. This is to say that what might be a joyful situation for one person may not necessarily be so for another.

Joy is expressed in various ways, but the most common are laughing and smiling, the latter being a restrained form of laughter. Some people respond to joy with a state of body relaxation. This is difficult to detect because it has little or no overt manifestation. However, it may be noticed when one compares it with body tension caused by unpleasant emotions.

As reported elsewhere, my studies show that a large majority of children derive the joyful experience of *fun* from participating in sports. The next three experiences of joy from sports are: (1) keeping my body fit, (2) winning, and (3) team spirit.

EMOTIONAL NEEDS OF CHILDREN

It has already been mentioned that it was a relatively easy matter to identify specific components of physical fitness. This did not hold true for social fitness, and neither does it hold true for emotional fitness. Therefore, in the absence of definitive components of emotional fitness, we need to look in other directions in our efforts to help children maintain satisfactory levels of emotional fitness.

Emotional maturity, and, hence, emotional fitness could be expressed in terms of the fulfillment of certain emotional needs. These needs can be reflected in the developmental characteristics of growing children. A number of emotional characteristics are identified in the following lists at the different age levels.

Five-Year-Old Children

1. Seldom shows jealousy toward younger siblings.
2. Usually sees only one way to do a thing.
3. Usually sees only one answer to a question.
4. Inclined not to change plans in the middle of an activity, but would rather begin over.
5. May fear being deprived of mother.
6. Some definite personality traits evidenced.
7. Is learning to get along better, but still may resort to quarreling and fighting.
8. Likes to be trusted with errands.
9. Enjoys performing simple tasks.
10. Wants to please and do what is expected of him.
11. Is beginning to sense right and wrong in terms of specific situations.

Six-Year-Old Children

1. Restless and may have difficulty in making decisions.
2. Emotional pattern of anger may be difficult to control at times.
3. Behavior patterns may often be explosive and unpredictable.
4. Jealousy toward siblings at times; at other times takes pride in siblings.
5. Greatly excited by anything new.
6. Behavior susceptible to shifts in direction, inwardly motivated, and outwardly stimulated.
7. May be self-assertive and dramatic.

Seven-Year-Old Children

1. Curiosity and creative desires may condition responses.
2. May be difficult to take criticism from adults.
3. Wants to be more independent.
4. Reaching for new experiences and trying to relate himself to enlarged world.
5. Overanxious to reach goals set by parents and teachers.
6. Critical of himself and sensitive to failure.
7. Emotional pattern of anger is more controlled.
8. Becoming less impulsive and boisterous in actions than at six.

Eight-Year-Old Children

1. Dislikes taking much criticism from adults.
2. Can give and take criticism in his own group.
3. May develop enemies.
4. Does not like to be treated as a child.
5. Has a marked sense of humor.
6. First impulse is to blame others.
7. Becoming more realistic and wants to find out for himself.

Nine-Year-Old Children

1. May sometimes be outspoken and critical of the adults he knows, although he has a genuine fondness for them.
2. Responds best to adults who treat him as an individual and approach him in an adult way.
3. Likes recognition for what he has done and responds well to deserved praise.
4. Likely to be backward about public recognition, but likes private praise.
5. Developing sympathy and loyalty to others.
6. Does not mind criticism or punishment if he thinks it is fair, but is indignant if he thinks it is unfair.
7. Disdainful of danger to and safety of himself, which may be a result of increasing interest in activities involving challenges and adventure.

Ten-Year-Old Children

1. Increasing tendency to rebel against adult domination.
2. Capable of loyalties and hero worship, and he can inspire it in his school mates.
3. Can be readily inspired to group loyalties in his club organization.
4. Likes the sense of solidarity that comes from keeping a group secret as a member of a group.
5. Each sex has an increasing tendency to show lack of sympathy and understanding with the other.
6. Boys' and girls' behavior and interest becoming increasingly different.

Eleven-Year-Old Children

1. If unskilled in group games and game skills, he may tend to withdraw.
2. Boys may be concerned if they feel they are underdeveloped.
3. May appear to be indifferent and uncooperative.
4. Moods change quickly.
5. Wants to grow up, but may be afraid to leave childhood security behind.
6. Increase in self-direction and in a serious attitude toward work.
7. Need for approval to feel secure.
8. Beginning to have a fully developed idea of own importance.

Twelve-Year-Old Children

1. Beginning to develop a truer picture of morality.
2. Clearer understanding of real causal relations.
3. The process of sexual maturation involves structured and physiological changes with possible perplexing and disturbing emotional problems.
4. Personal appearance may become a source of great conflict, and learning to appreciate good grooming or the reverse may be prevalent.
5. May be very easily hurt when criticized or made the scapegoat.
6. Maladjustment may occur when there is not a harmonious relationship between child and adults.

It should be obvious that the above emotional characteristics reflect some of the emotional needs of children at the different age levels. These characteristics should be taken into account in the sports situation if we expect to meet with success in meeting these needs.

GUIDELINES FOR EMOTIONAL DEVELOPMENT THROUGH SPORTS

Guidelines for emotional development are set forth here in the same manner that guidelines for physical and social development through sports were proposed in the two previous chapters; that is, these guidelines take the form of valid *concepts of emotional development.* When we have a basis for the emotional behavior of children as they grow and develop, we are then in a better position to provide sports experiences that are likely to be compatible with emotional development. The following list of concepts of emotional development with implications for children's sports are submitted with this general idea in mind.

1. **An Emotional Response May Be Brought About by a Goal's Being Furthered or Thwarted.** The coach should make a very serious effort to assure successful sports experiences for every child. This can be accomplished in part by attempting to provide for individual differences within given sports experiences. The sports setting should be such that each child derives a feeling of personal worth through making some sort of positive contribution.

2. **Self-Realization Experiences Should be Constructive.** The opportunity for creative experience inherent in sports affords the child an excellent chance for self-realization through physical expression. Coaches might consider planning with children themselves to see that activities are meeting their needs and, as a result, involve a constructive experience.

3. **Emotional Responses Increase as the Development of the Child Brings Greater Awareness, the Ability to Remember the Past and to Anticipate the Future.** The coach can remind the children of their past emotional responses with words of praise. This should encourage children to repeat such responses in future similar sports situations.

4. **As the Child Develops, the Emotional Reactions Tend to Become Less Violent and More Discriminating.** A well-planned program and progressive sequence of sports experiences can provide for release of aggression in a socially acceptable manner.

5. **Emotional Reactions Displayed in Early Childhood Are Likely to be Continued in Some Form in Later Years.** This could be one of the best reasons for providing sports experiences for children. Through sports experiences in the formative years we can help children develop constructive emotional reactions through a medium that they understand best—body movement. Through the spontaneous freedom of expression of emotional reactions in the sports experience, the real feelings of the child are more easily identified.

6. **Emotional Reactions Tend to Increase Beyond Normal Expectancy Toward the Constructive or Destructive on the Balance of Furthering or Hindering Experiences of the Child.** For some children, the confidence they need to be able to face the problems of life may come about through sports. Therefore, sports have tremendous potential to help contribute toward a solid base of total development.

7. **Depending on Certain Factors, A Child's Own Feelings May Be Accepted or Rejected by the Individual.** Children's sports experiences

should make them feel good and have confidence in themselves. Satisfactory self-concept is closely related to body control; therefore sports experiences might be considered as one of the best ways of contributing to it.

OPPORTUNITIES FOR EMOTIONAL DEVELOPMENT THROUGH SPORTS

Coaches have tended to give generous praise to sports for their potential to provide for emotional stability. The extent to which this actually accrues is dependent primarily upon the kind of emotional climate provided by the coach and the sports experiences provided for the children. For this reason it appears pertinent to examine some of the opportunities that exist for emotional development through sports.

1. **Release of Aggression in a Socially Acceptable Manner.** This appears to be an outstanding way in which sports experiences can help to make children more secure and emotionally stable. For example, kicking a ball in a game of soccer or batting a baseball can afford a socially acceptable way of releasing aggression.

2. **Inhibition of Direct Response of Unpleasant Emotions.** This statement does not necessarily mean that feelings concerned with such unpleasant emotions as fear and anger should be completely restrained. On the contrary, the interpretation should be that such feelings can take place less frequently in a good sports situation. This means that opportunities can be provided to relieve tension rather than to aggravate it.

3. **Promotion of Pleasant Emotions.** Perhaps there is too much concern with suppressing unpleasant emotions and not enough attention given to the promotion of pleasant ones. One of the glorious things about sports is that the range of activities is so great that there is "something for everybody." Thus, all children regardless of ability should be afforded the opportunity for success, at least some of the time.

4. **Freedom From Fear.** This depends largely upon the approach taken by the coach. As mentioned previously, when discussing a gymnastic activity, if the coach says, "If you do it that way you will break your neck," such a negative approach can instill a fear that may not have existed originally. It is also well to remember that "getting hurt" is a fear that many children have about sports.

5. **Recognition of One's Abilities and Limitations.** It has already been mentioned that the wide range of activities in sports as well as different

positions played should provide an opportunity for success for all. This should make it easier to provide for individual differences of children so that all of them can progress within the limits of their own skill and ability.

6. **Understanding About the Ability and Achievements of Others.** In the sports experience, emphasis can be placed upon the achievement of the group along with the function of each individual in the group. Team play is the basis of many sports activities.

7. **Being Able to Make a Mistake Without Being Ostracized.** This requires that the coach serve as a catalyst who helps children understand the idea of trial and error. Emphasis can be placed on "trying" and that one can learn not only from his or her own mistakes, but from the mistakes of others as well.

The above discussion includes just a few examples of the numerous opportunities to help provide for emotional development through sports. The resourceful and creative coach will be able to expand this list manyfold. It bears repeating that emotional development through sports will not accrue automatically. Although sports theoretically provide a near-ideal setting for children to react in terms of ordinary behavior instead of highly emotional behavior, this situation does not always prevail. For instance, in cases where children are placed under stress in highly competitive situations over prolonged periods, there may be a strong possibility of detraction from, rather than a contribution to, their emotional stability.

IMPLICATIONS OF RESEARCH IN EMOTIONAL BEHAVIOR OF CHILDREN

It was mentioned in the preceding chapter that in a documentary analysis of research reported in the *Research Quarterly of Exercise and Sports,* only 12 percent of these studies were concerned in some way with the emotional aspect of personality. Moreover, for the most part, these studies are not very definitive in terms of validity of the findings. This being the case, we can again turn to some of the psychological research that has been conducted in emotional development so that we might draw some implications for sports. Reference is made again to the report of the National Institute of Education, which was mentioned in the preceding chapter. The following is a list of generalizations derived from the findings reported in the study of *aggression* in children and are accompanied by possible general implications for sports. These implications are suggestive only, and the reader will no doubt be able to draw his or her own implications and make practical applications that apply to particular situations.

1. **Sufficient Space May Eliminate Accidental Pushing and Shoving That Can Lead to Retaliatory Aggression.** The implication for sports practice sessions should be obvious in that movement requires space in which to move. There are two situations concerned with space. These are the amount of space required to perform a particular movement and the utilization of available space. With regard to the latter it has been suggested that young children, during nonstructured, self-initiated play, seem to reveal differences in the quantity of space they use and that these differences may be associated in important ways with other aspects of the child's development. Some studies tend to support the concept that space utilization of the young child in active play is a relatively stable dimension of his patterned behavior.

2. **Children Rewarded for Aggression Learn That Aggression Pays Off.** This generalization is concerned with the extent to which a coach uses praise for achievement. The coach must be able to quickly discern whether success was due to more aggressive behavior than skill. The important thing here is the extent of aggressive behavior. Certainly a coach should not thwart enthusiasm. It is sometimes difficult to determine whether an act was due to genuine enthusiasm or overt undesirable aggressive behavior.

3. **Children Involved in Constructive Activities May Be Less Likely to Behave Aggressively.** This implies that sports practice sessions should be well planned so that time is spent on constructive sports activities. When this is accomplished it will be more likely that desirable and more worthwhile learning will take place.

4. **Children Who Have Alternative Responses Readily Available Are Less Likely to Resort to Aggression to Get What They Want.** This is essentially concerned with coach-player relationships. While sports generally involve group situations, there are many "one-on-one" opportunities between the coach and child. This gives the coach a chance to verbalize to the child the kind of behavior that is expected under certain conditions. For example, a child who asks for an object such as a ball is more likely to receive cooperation. On the other hand, a child who grabs an object is more likely to elicit retaliatory aggression. Coach reinforce-

ment can increase children's use of nonaggressive solutions to interpersonal problems.

The coach should be ready to intervene in a potentially aggressive situation before aggression occurs, encouraging children to use nonaggressive methods to solve conflicts. The coach can provide verbal alternatives for those children who do not think of them for themselves. For example, "I am playing with this now," or "You can ask him to trade with you."

5. **Children Imitate Behavior of People They Like, and They Often Adopt a Coach's Behavior.** Coaches are more likely to be a model adopted by children than would be the case with most other adults—even including some parents. One of the reasons is that coaches meet children on a much more informal basis. In addition, they deal with children in an area that is less inhibiting to children and one that is much more likely to be "fun-oriented." Coaches can take advantage of this situation by being nonaggressive in their own behaviors.

6. **Cooperation May Be Incompatible With Aggression.** This could be interpreted to mean that the coach should consistently attend to and reinforce all cooperative behavior. Children consistently reinforced for cooperative behavior are likely to increase cooperative interactions while simultaneously decreasing aggressive behavior.

EVALUATING CONTRIBUTIONS OF SPORTS TO EMOTIONAL DEVELOPMENT

When we attempt to evaluate the emotional aspect of personality, we tend to encounter much the same situation as when we attempt to evaluate the social aspect. Included among some of the methods used for attempting to measure emotional responses are:

1. Blood pressure (it rises when one is under some sort of emotional stress).
2. Blood sugar analysis (under stressful conditions more sugar enters the blood stream).
3. Pulse rate (emotional stress causes it to elevate).
4. Galvanic skin response (similar to the lie detector technique, and measurements are recorded in terms of perspiration in palms of hands).

These as well as others that have been used by investigators of human emotion have various and perhaps limited egrees of validity. In attempting to assess emotional reactivity, we oftentimes encounter the problem of the extent to which we are dealing with a purely physiological response or a purely emotional response. For example, one's pulse rate could be elevated by taking some sort of physical exercise. It could likewise be elevated if a person were the object of an embarrassing remark by another person. Thus, in this illustration the elevation of pulse rate could be caused by different reasons; the first being physiological and the second, emotional.

I can also illustrate this with an experiment that I conducted several years ago. At the time I was proclaiming that the game of *golf* was much more emotional than physical: that is, "You can't raise a pulse rate with a putt." I had ten sixth-grade boys stand around the edge of a large green to see which one could "get down" in the least number of strokes. Pulse rates were taken just before and after the activity. For most of the boys there was little or no rise in pulse rate. The next step was to offer a prize of one dollar to the winner. Pulse rates were again taken for each boy and a considerable rise occurred. By introducing the "emotional variable" I was able to show the difference between a purely physiological response and a purely emotional response.

Another consideration to take into account is that the type of emotional pattern is not identified by the measuring device; that is, a joy response and an anger response could show the same or nearly the same rise in pulse rate. These are some of the reasons why it is most difficult to arrive at a high degree of objectivity in studying the emotional aspect of personality.

What we are essentially concerned with here is how an individual coach can make some sort of valid evaluation of the extent to which sports contribute to emotional development. This means that the coach should make some attempt to assess sports experiences with reference to whether or not these experiences are providing for emotional maturity.

One such approach would be to refer back to the list of "opportunities for emotional development through sports" suggested earlier in this chapter. I have converted these opportunities into a rating scale as follows:

1. The sports experience provides for release of aggression in a socially acceptable manner.

   4—most of the time
   3—some of the time
   2—occasionally
   1—infrequently

2. The sports experience provides for inhibition of direct response of unpleasant emotions.

   4—most of the time
   3—some of the time
   2—occasionally
   1—infrequently

3. The sports experience provides for promotion of pleasant emotion.

   4—most of the time
   3—some of the time
   2—occasionally
   1—infrequently

4. The sports experience provides for freedom from fear.

   4—most of the time
   3—some of the time
   2—occasionally
   1—infrequently

5. The sports experience provides for recognition of one's abilities and limitations.

   4—most of the time
   3—some of the time
   2—occasionally
   1—infrequently

6. The sports experience provides for an understanding about the ability and achievement of others.

   4—most of the time
   3—some of the time
   2—occasionally
   1—infrequently

7. The sports experience provides for being able to make a mistake without being ostracized.

   4—most of the time
   3—some of the time
   2—occasionally
   1—infrequently

If the coach or parent makes these rating objectively and conscientiously, a reasonably good procedure for evaluation is provided. Ratings can be made periodically to see if positive changes appear to be taking place. Ratings can be made for a single sports experience, a group of sports experiences, or for an entire season. This procedure can help the coach and parent identify the extent to which sports experiences and/or conditions under which the experiences take place are contributing to emotional development.

Chapter 6

INTELLECTUAL DEVELOPMENT OF CHILDREN THROUGH SPORTS

It has been stated previously that of the contributions sports make to the total development of the child, the one concerned with intellectual development has been subjected to a great deal of criticism by some. It has been demonstrated, however, that there are many potential opportunities for intellectual development through the medium of sports. It will be a major function of this chapter to set forth some of these potential possibilities.

INTELLECTUAL NEEDS OF CHILDREN

In Chapter 2, on a discussion of intellectual fitness, the point was made that children have certain general intellectual needs: (1) a need for challenging experiences at the child's level of ability, (2) a need for intellectually successful and satisfying experiences, (3) a need for the opportunity to solve problems, and (4) a need for the opportunity to participate in creative experiences instead to always having to conform.

As in the case of physical, social, and emotional needs, children have certain specific intellectual needs. These specific needs can be reflected in the developmental characteristics of children. A number of intellectual characteristics are identified in the following lists at the different age levels.

Five-Year-Old Children

1. Enjoys copying designs, letters, and numbers.
2. Interested in completing tasks.
3. May tend to monopolize table conversation.
4. Memory for past events good.
5. Looks at books and pretends to read.
6. Likes recordings, words, and music that tell a story.

7. Enjoys counting objects.
8. Over 2,000 words in speaking vocabulary.
9. Can speak in complete sentences.
10. Can sing simple melodies, beat good rhythms, and recognize simple tunes.
11. Daydreams seem to center around make-believe play.
12. Attention span increasing up to 20 minutes in some cases.
13. Is able to plan activities.
14. Enjoys stories, dramatic plays, and poems.
15. Enjoys making up dances to music.
16. Pronunciation is usually clear.
17. Can express needs well in words.

Six-Year-Old Children

1. Speaking vocabulary of over 2,500 words.
2. Interest span inclined to be short.
3. Knows number combinations up to ten.
4. Knows comparative values of the common coins.
5. Can define objects in terms of what they are used for.
6. Knows right and left side of body.
7. Has an association with creative activity and motorized life experience.
8. Drawings are crude but realistic and suggestive of early man.
9. Will contribute to guided group planning.
10. Conversation usually concerns own experience and interests.
11. Curiosity is active and memory is strong.
12. Identifies self with imaginary characters.

Seven-Year-Old Children

1. Abstract thinking is barely beginning.
2. Is able to listen longer.
3. Reads some books by himself.
4. Is able to reason, but has little experience upon which to base judgments.
5. The attention span is still short and retention poor, but does not object to repetition.
6. Reaction time is still slow.
7. Learning to evaluate the achievements of self and others.

8. Concerned with own lack of skill and achievement.
9. Becoming more realistic and less imaginative.

Eight-Year-Old Children

1. Can tell day of month and year.
2. Voluntary attention span increasing.
3. Interested in far-off places, and ways of communication now have real meaning.
4. Becoming more aware of adult world and his place in it.
5. Ready to tackle almost anything.
6. Shows a capacity for self-evaluation.
7. Likes to memorize.
8. Not always too good at telling time, but very much aware of it.

Nine-Year-Old Children

1. Individual differences are clear and distinct.
2. Some real interests are beginning to develop.
3. Beginning to have a strong sense of right and wrong.
4. Understands explanations.
5. Interests are closer to ten- or eleven-year-olds than to seven- or eight-year-olds.
6. As soon as a project fails to hold interest, it may be dropped without further thought.
7. Attention span is greatly increased.
8. Seems to be guided best by a reason, simple and clear cut, for a decision that needs to be made.
9. Ready to learn from occasional failure of his judgment as long as learning takes place in situations where failure will not have too serious consequences.
10. Able to make up own mind and come to decisions.
11. Marked reading disabilities begin to be more evident and may tend to influence the personality.
12. Range of interest in reading in that many are great readers while others may be barely interested in books.
13. Will average between six and seven words per remark.

Ten-Year-Old Children

1. Works with executive speed and likes the challenge of mathematics.
2. Shows a capacity to budget time and energy.
3. Can attend to a visual task and at the same time maintain conversation.
4. Some become discouraged and may give up trying when unsuccessful.
5. The attention span has lengthened considerably, with the child able to listen and to follow directions and retain knowledge more easily.
6. Beginning understanding of real causal relations.
7. Making finer conceptual distinctions and thinking reflectively.
8. Developing a scientific approach.
9. Better oriented with respect to time.
10. Ready to plan his day and accept responsibility for getting things done on time.

Eleven-Year-Old Children

1. Increasing power of attention.
2. Able to maintain a longer period of intellectual activity between firsthand experiences.
3. Interested in scientific experiments and procedures.
4. Can carry on many individual intellectual responsibilities.
5. Able to discuss problems and to see different side of questions.
6. May lack maturity of judgment.
7. Increased language facility.
8. Attention span is increasing, and concentration may be given to a task for a long period of time.
9. Level of aspiration has increased.
10. Growing in ability to use several facts to make a decision.
11. Insight into causal relationships is developing more and is manifested by many how and why questions.

Twelve-Year-Old Children

1. Learns more ways of studying and controlling the physical world.
2. The use of language (on many occasions his own vocabulary) to exchange ideas for explanatory reasons.
3. More use of reflective thinking and greater ease of distinction.
4. Continuation in development of scientific approach.

It should be obvious that the above intellectual characteristics of children of different ages should be taken into account if we are to meet with any degree of success in our efforts in the direction of intellectual development through sports.

GUIDELINES FOR INTELLECTUAL DEVELOPMENT THROUGH SPORTS

Guidelines for intellectual development are set forth here in the same manner that guidelines for physical, social, and emotional development through sports were proposed in previous chapters; that is, these guidelines take the form of valid *concepts of intellectual development.* When we have some sort of basis for intellectual behavior of children as they grow and develop, we are then in a better position to provide sports experiences that are likely to be compatible with intellectual development. The following list of concepts of intellectual development with implications for children's sports are submitted with this general idea in mind.

1. **Children Differ in Intelligence.** Coaches and parents should be aware that poor performance of some children in sports activities might be due to the fact that they have difficulty with communication. Differences in intelligence levels as well as physical skill and ability need to be taken into account in the planning of sports practice sessions.

2. **Intelligence Develops Through the Interaction of the Child and His or Her environment.** Body movement experiences in sports involve a process of interaction with the environment. There are many problem-solving opportunities in the well-planned sports environment, and thus the child can be presented with challenging learning situations.

3. **Emotional Stress May Affect Measures of Intelligence.** Sports experiences have potential value in the relief of emotional stress. This can possibly make the child more effective from an intellectual point of view.

4. **Extremes in Intelligence Show Differences in Personality Characteristics.** The coach should be aware of the range of intelligence of children in a particular group. Experiences should be provided that challenge the so-called gifted child as well as meeting the needs of those children who are below average. In the sports experience, children can learn to respect individual differences as far as levels of intelligence are concerned.

5. **The Child's Self-Concept of His or Her Ability to Deal with Intellectual Tasks Influences His or Her Successful Dealing With Such Tasks.** The sports experiences should contain a large degree of variation (playing

different position on a team). This way it will likely insure that all children will achieve success at one time or another.

OPPORTUNITIES FOR INTELLECTUAL
DEVELOPMENT THROUGH SPORTS

The idea that participation in sports can contribute to a child's intellectual development is not necessarily new. For example, over 23 centuries ago Plato, the famous Greek philosopher, postulated in *The Republic:* "No compulsion my good friend . . . in teaching children, train them by a kind of game, and you will be able to see more clearly the natural bent of each." Shortly after the turn of the present century in her famous book on games Jessie H. Bancroft commented that "As a child's perceptions are quickened, he sees more quickly that the ball is coming toward him, that he is in danger of being tagged, or that it is his turn; he hears footsteps behind him, or his name or number called; he feels the touch on the shoulder; or in innumerable other ways he is aroused to the quick and direct recognition of, and response to, things that go on around him."

It is the general opinion of most learning theorists that problem solving is the major way of human learning; that is, learning can take place well when problem-solving opportunities are provided. In a well-planned sports situation there are numerous opportunities for children to exercise judgment and resort to reflective thinking in the solution of various kinds of problems. In addition, children must acquire a knowledge of rules and regulations for various games. It is also important for effective participation that children gain an understanding of the various fundamentals and strategies involved in the performance of sports activities.

Another very important aspect of intellectual development in sports is that which is concerned with the extent to which children can improve upon their *listening* skills. In this particular connection, it has been observed that in the auditory-input phase of a sports teaching-learning situation children "attend to" better than they do in this phase of a lesson in school subject areas. This means that in a well-planned sports learning situation, the child's attention is likely to be focused on the learning task and learning behavior. (This will be discussed in detail in Chapter 8).

Improving Perceptual-Motor Development Through Sports

Perception is concerned with how we obtain information from the environment through the various sensory modalities and what we make of it. In the present context *motor* is concerned with the impulse for motion resulting in a change of position through the various forms of body movement. When the two terms are put together (perceptual-motor) the implication is an organization of interpretation of sensory data, with related voluntary motor responses

Perceptual-motor development involves the correction, or at least some degree of improvement of certain motor deficiencies, especially those associated with fine motor coordination. What some specialists have identified as a "perceptual-motor deficit" syndrome is said to exist with certain neurologically handicapped children. An attempt may be made to correct or improve fine motor control problems through a carefully developed sequence of motor competencies which follow a definite hierarchy of development. This may occur through a structured perceptual-motor program which is likely to be dependent upon a series of systematic exercises. Or, it can occur through participation in certain sports with attempts to provide for these corrections or improvements when children engage in sports activities where perceptual-motor developmental factors may be inherent. This procedure (sports participation) is much more fun for children and at the same time is more likely to be free from emotionally traumatizing situations sometimes attendant in some highly-structured perceptual-motor programs.

Perceptual-Motor Skills

There is a considerable amount of agreement among child development specialists that there is no simple distinction between a perceptual skill and a motor skill. This has, no doubt, led to the term *perceptual-motor skills.* In fact, to some extent this term may have supplanted such terms as *neuromuscular* and *sensorimotor.*

In general, the postulation appears to be that if perceptual training improves perceptual and motor abilities, then, because of the fact that perceptual and motor abilities are so highly interrelated and interdependent upon each other, it follows that training in perception should alleviate perceptual-motor problems. There is objective support for the idea that perceptual training can improve perceptual ability. Although there is not a great deal of clear-cut evidence to support the idea that perceptual-motor training does increase the performance of perceptual-motor skills, some research has indicated that certain perceptual-motor skills can be significantly improved for certain children under certain conditions.

What then are the perceptual-motor skills? Generally, the kinds of skills that fit into a combination of manual coordination and eye-hand skills may be considered a valid classification.

Visual perception is based on sensorimotor experiences that depend on visual acuity, eye-hand coordination, left-right body orientation, and other visual spatial abilities, including visual sequencing. Some studies have shown a positive correlation between difficulties in visual perception and achievement in reading.

Indications of a child's eye-hand coordination may be observed as he or she bounces or throws a ball. It has been indicated that in reading, the child shows difficulty in eye-hand coordination by his inability to keep his place in reading, to find the place again in the pattern of printed words, and to maintain the motor adjustment as long as is necessary to comprehend a word, a phrase, or a sentence. His tendency to skip lines arises from an inability to direct his eyes accurately to the beginning of the next line.

Depending upon a variety of extenuating circumstances, perceptual-motor skills require a degree of voluntary action. The basic striking and catching skills are examples of this type and are important in certain kinds of team games; that is, receiving an object (catching) such as a ball, and hitting (striking) an object, ordinarily with an implement, such as batting a ball.

There are tasks perceptual-motor in character, that are accomplished with one hand. At a high level of performance this could involve receiving a ball with one hand in a highly organized sports activity such as baseball. At a very low level, a baby will reach for an object or grasp an object with one hand.

In some kinds of visual tasks requiring the use of one eye, there appears to be an eye preference. In reading, it is believed that one eye may lead or be dominant. In tasks where one eye is used and one hand is used, most people will use those on the same side of the body. This is to say that there is *lateral dominance.* In the case of those who use the left eye and right hand or the opposite of this *mixed dominance* is said to exist. Some studies suggest that mixed dominance may have a negative effect on motor coordination, but perhaps just as many investigators report that this is not the case.

The development of perceptual-motor abilities in children is referred to by some child development specialists as the process of providing "learning to learn" activities. This means improvement upon such perceptual-motor qualities as *body awareness, laterality and directionality* (sense of direction), *auditory and visual perception skills,* and *kinesthetic and tactile perception skills.* A deficiency in one or more of these can detract from a child's ability to learn.

It will be the function of the following discussions to help coaches and parents determine if such deficiencies exist, along with how participation in certain sports experiences help improve upon them. Even though a deficiency does not exist in any of these factors, the sports experiences suggested can still be used to sharpen and improve upon these skills which are so important to learning.

Body Awareness

The best description that I have seen of *body awareness* is that given by British Sports Psychologist Whiting and his associates[1] over two decades ago. They described it as: "an appreciation and understanding of the body as an instrument of movement and vehicle of expression in nonverbal communication."

It is doubtful that there are any absolutely foolproof methods of detecting problems of body awareness in children. The reason for this is that many mannerisms said to be indicative of body-awareness problems can be symptomatic of other deficiencies. Nevertheless, those persons such as coaches and parents who deal with children should be alert to detect certain possible deficiencies. One way to detect body-awareness problems is to observe certain behaviors. The following generalized list contains examples of such behaviors and is submitted to assist the reader in this particular regard.

1. Sometimes the child with a lack of body awareness may manifest tenseness in his or her movements. At the same time the child may be unsure of his or her movements in attempting to move the body segments.

---

[1]Whiting, H. T. A., et al, *Personality and Performance in Physical Education and Sport,* London, Henry Kimpton, 1973.

2. If the child is instructed to move a body part such as placing one foot forward, the child may direct attention to the body part before making the movement. Or, he or she may look at another child to observe the movement before attempting to make the movement. This could be due to poor processing of the input (auditory or visual) provided for the movement.

3. When instructed to use one body part (arm) the child may also move the corresponding body part (other arm) when it is not necessary. For example, the child may be asked to swing the right arm and he or she may also start to swing the left arm simultaneously.

4. In such activities as catching a ball the child may turn toward the ball when this is not necessary. For example, when a basketball thrown to the child approaches close to him or her, the child may move forward with either side of the body rather than trying to retrieve the ball with the hands while both feet remain stationary.

In general, it might be said that when a child is given the opportunity to use the body freely in enjoyable movement such as sports, an increase in body awareness occurs. In games that require running, such as football, baseball, basketball and soccer, the importance of the feet and legs is recognized. Games that require the use of the hands and arms are useful in the identification of the upper extremities. Thus, there are many opportunities in sports activities to improve upon the child's body awareness.

Laterality and Directionality

Laterality and directionality are concerned with distinction of the body sides and sense of direction. More specifically, laterality is an internal awareness of the left and right sides of the body in relation to the child himself. It is concerned with the child's knowledge of how each side of the body is used separately or together. Directionality is the projection into space of laterality; that is, the awareness of left and right, up and down, over and under, etc. in the world around the child. Stated in another way, directionality in space is the ability to project outside the body the laterality that the child has developed within himself.

The categories of laterality and directionality make up the broader classification of *directional awareness.* The development of this quality is most important, in that it is an essential element for reading and writing.

These two basic Rs require the hand and/or eyes to move from left to right in a coordinated manner. Also, interpretation of left and right direction is an important requirement for the child in dealing with the environment. It is interesting to note that some children who have not developed laterality quite often will write numbers sequentially from left to right. However, when doing addition and subtraction, they may want to start from the left instead of the right.

Since laterality and directionality are inherent aspects of body awareness, some of the methods of detecting deficiencies in body awareness mentioned previously apply here. In addition, it may be noted that the child is inclined to use the dominant side of the body. Also, confusion may result if the child is given directions for body movement which call for a specific direction in which he or she is to move.

In activities that require running to a given point such as a base, the child may tend to veer away from it. Or, the child may not perceive the position of other children in a game such as basketball and, as a consequence, may run into them frequently. These are factors that coaches and parents can observe in children in their sports environment.

Generally speaking, a relatively large number of sports activities involve some aspect of lateralness, while a more moderate number are concerned with directionality. Some sports activities involve *unilateral* movements; those performed with one side or part of the body (throwing with the dominant arm). Some sports involve *bilateral* movement. This means that both sides or segments of the body are in action simultaneously in the same manner, such as the two-hand shot in basketball. *Cross-lateral* movement is involved when segments of the body are used simultaneously but in a different manner (running and dribbling a basketball). Many activities are concerned with changing direction which is likely to involve directionality, (any sport that requires dodging).

Sometimes it is useful to engage in certain kinds of drill in practice to provide for laterality and directionality; for example, the *ZigZag Run* which is performed as follows.

A group is divided into teams. The teams form rows behind a starting line. Four ten pins or other objects, are placed in a line four feet apart in front of each team. On a signal, the first child on each team runs to the right of the first pin and to the left of the second pin, and so on, in a zigzag fashion, going around the last pin. The child returns to place in the same manner. The second child proceeds as the first child. If a child knocks down a pin that child must set it up before continuing. The team finishing first wins. This activity gives children practice in changing direction as they run around the objects. The coach can observe closely to notice the children who are having difficulty in performing the task. This practice can carry over into more complex sports activities that require dodging as is the case of a forward trying to elude a guard in basketball.

Kinesthetic Perception

Kinesthesis, the kinesthetic sense, has been described in many ways. Some definitions of the term are somewhat comprehensive while others are less so. One comprehensive definition of kinesthesis is that it is the sense which enables us to determine the position of the segments of the body, their rate, extent, and direction of movement, the position of the entire body, and the characteristics of total body motion. Another, less complicated description of the term characterizes it as the sense that tells the individual where his body is and how it moves.

In summarizing the many definitions of the term the following four factors seem to be constant, thus emphasizing the likenesses of the many definitions of the term: (1) position of the body segments, (2) precision of movement, (3) balance, and (4) space orientation. For the discussion here I will think of kinesthetic perception as the *mental interpretation of the sensation of body movement.*

Although there are a number of specific test items that are supposed to measure kinesthesis, the use of such tests may be of questionable value in diagnosing deficiencies in children. Therefore, my recommendation is that coaches and parents resort to the observation of certain behaviors and mannerisms of children, using some simple diagnostics to determine deficiencies in kinesthetic sensitivity.

Various authorities on the subject suggest that children with kinesthetic problems possess certain characteristics that may be identifying factors. For example, it has been indicated that a child who is deficient in kinesthetic sensitivity will likely be clumsy, awkward, and inefficient in his or her movements and impaired in getting acquainted with the handling of the world of objects. A child who has difficulty in the use of his or her hands or the body in attempting to perform unfamiliar tasks involving body movement can no doubt benefit from activities involving kinesthesis.

With reference to the above, coaches and parents should be on the alert to observe a child who has difficulty with motor coordination; that is, using the muscles in such a manner that they work together effectively. Such lack of coordination may be seen in children who have difficulty in performing the movement skills that involved an uneven rhythm such as *skipping.* Coaches and parents can observe these deficiencies in the normal movement activities of children, and a skill such as skipping can be used as a diagnostic technique in identifying such problems. (Skipping and other locomotor skills will be discussed in detail in the following chapter.)

Since balance is an important aspect of kinesthesis, simple tests for balance can be administered to determine if there is a lack of proficiency. One such test is to have the child stand on either foot. Ordinarily, a child should be able to maintain such a position for a period of at least five seconds.

Since kinesthetic sensitivity is concerned with the sensation of movement and orientation of the body in space, it is not an easy matter to isolate specific activities suited *only* for this purpose. The reason for this, of course, is that practically all of these activities involve total or near total physical response. However, activities that make the child particularly aware of the movement of certain muscle groups, as well as those where resistance is encountered, are of particular value in helping the child develop a kinesthetic awareness of his or her body. Many sports activities provide these qualities that will improve the child' kinesthetic sensitivity. The following game of *Rush and Tug* can be used in practice sessions for sports activities to sharpen children's kinesthetic sensitivity.

In this activity there are two groups with each group standing between one of two parallel lines which are about 40 feet apart. In the middle of these two parallel lines is a rope laid perpendicular to them. A cloth is tied to the middle of the rope to designate both halves of the rope. On a signal, members of both groups rush to their half of the rope, pick it up and tug toward the other group's end line. The group pulling the midpoint of the rope past its own end line in a specified amount of time is the winner. If, at the end of the designated time, the midpoint of the rope has not been pulled beyond either group's line, the group with the midpoint of the rope nearer to its end is the winner. In this activity the children can be reminded of the resistance they are experiencing as they try to pull the opposing group; also, the experience of feeling the muscle groups of the arms and legs working together.

Tactile Perception

The tactile sense is very closely related to the kinesthetic sense; so much so, in fact, that these two senses are often confused. One of the main reasons for this is that the ability to detect changes in touch (tactile) involves many of the same receptors concerned with informing the body of changes in its position. The essential difference between the tactile sense and the kinesthetic sense may be seen in the definitions of kinesthetic and tactile perception. As stated previously, kinesthetic perception involves the mental interpretation of the sensation of body movement, whereas tactile perception is concerned with the *mental interpretation of what a person experiences through the sense of touch.*

Since the kinesthetic and tactile senses are so closely related, the identifying factors of deficiency in kinesthesis previously reported can also be used to determine if there is a deficiency in the tactile sense.

Many sports activities provide for tactile sensitivity. For example, dribbling a basketball gives the feeling of the ball movement and its placement on the floor. This also has value as far as *timing* is related to kinesthetic perception. The sport of wrestling, by providing body-to-body contact, has a high level of tactile sensitivity. Also, gymnastic activities that have the child come in contact with the surface area or a piece of apparatus have this same quality.

At a very high level of sports activity—professional football—the television viewer will perhaps have noticed that two or more offensive linemen (not on the home team) will be holding hands. The reason for this is that the players away from the center cannot hear the quarterback's signals because of the crowd noise. At the snap of the ball the inside lineman will release the hand of his teammate. In this situation the tactile sense becomes a medium of communication.

Visual and Auditory Perception

The visual and auditory systems provide two of the most important forms of input for learning. The term *visual* is concerned with images that are obtained through the eyes. Thus, visual input involves the various learning media directed to the visual sense. The term *auditory* may be described as stimulation occurring through the sense organs of hearing. Therefore, auditory input is concerned with the various learning media directed to the auditory sense.

These two forms of sensory input complement each other in individuals who have both normal vision and hearing. However, as the extremes away from normalcy are approached; that is, in the case of complete or near-complete absence of one of the senses, their use as combined learning media obviously diminishes. However, at the extremes of normalcy, a person relies a great deal upon the system which is functioning normally. For example, although the sightless person relies a great deal upon tactile perception, particularly as far as "reading" is concerned, he or she is also extremely sensitive to auditory input in the form of various sounds. In a like manner the hearing-impaired person relies heavily upon the visual sense as a form of sensory input.

The relationship of these two senses in children with normal or near-normal functioning of both senses is seen in the area of reading. That is, there is a natural sequence from listening to reading, and the acquisition of the skill of auditory discrimination is an important factor in learning to read. Additionally, in many sports teaching-learning situations these two forms of sensory input are used in combination; for example, the coach might use oral communication to describe shooting a basketball, demonstrating the skill at the same time. Of course, one of the important features for coaches to consider is the extent to which these aspects of sensory input should be used simultaneously. The coach needs to be aware of how well a certain group of children can handle two tasks together (explanation and demonstration). In other words, if visual and auditory input are combined in a sports teaching-learning situation, the coach must determine whether or not, and to what extent, one becomes an attention-distracting factor for the other.

Visual Perception

Visual perception is the mental interpretation of what a person sees. A number of aspects of visual perception that have been identified include eye-motor coordination, figure-ground perception, form constancy, position in space, and spatial relationships. It has been suggested that children who show deficiency in these various areas may have difficulty in school performance. Various training programs have been devised to help correct or improve these conditions in children, with the idea that such training would result in the improvement of learning ability. The extent to which this has been accomplished has been extolled by some but seriously questioned by others. Research involving this general type of training does not present clear-cut and definitive evidence to support the notion that such training result in academic achievement.

Any number of sports experiences provide for improvement of visual perception particularly as it is concerned with *visualization* and *visual motor coordination.* Visualization involves visual image, which is the mental construction of a visual experience, or the result of mentally combining a number of visual experiences. Visual-motor coordination is concerned with visual-motor tasks that involve the integration of vision and movement. Think about those sports where we are continually admonishing, "keep your eye on the ball," or "look the ball into your hands."

The following activities can be used for sports practice drills to help children improve on visual perception. And, again, these activities can carry over into the more complex sports activities.

In the game *Jump the Shot* the children form a circle, with one child standing in the center holding a length of rope with an object tied to one end. The object should be something soft such as a beanbag. The player in the center starts the game by swinging the object on the rope around and around close to the feet of the players forming the circle. The players in the circle attempt to avoid being hit by the object by jumping over it when it goes by them. A point can be scored against any person hit on the feet by the object on the rope. This activity provides a good opportunity for visual-motor coordination, as a child must quickly coordinate his or her movement with the visual experience. This can be a good evaluation technique for the coach since it can be seen how well a child makes the judgment necessary to jump over the object at the proper time.

In the game *Ball Pass,* the players are divided into two or more groups and each group forms a circle. The object of the game is to pass the ball around the circle to see which group can get it around first. The coach gives the directions for the ball to be passed or tossed from one player to another. For example, the coach may say, "Pass the ball to the right," "Toss the ball over two players," and so on. The game may be varied by using more than one ball of different sizes and weights. For instance, a basketball, volleyball, and tennis ball might be used. This activity provides a good opportunity to improve eye-hand coordination, and it has been observed that after practice in this activity poor coordination can be improved.

In *Keep It Up* children are divided into several small circles, with each circle having a basketball. On a signal, one child tosses the ball into the air and the other children try to see how long they can keep the ball up without letting it touch the surface area. The group that keeps it up in the air for the longest time is the winner. This activity can be used for the improvement of eye-hand coordination.

Auditory Perception

It was estimated several years ago that about 75 percent of the waking hours is spent in verbal communication—45 percent in listening, 30 percent in speaking, 16 percent in reading and the remaining 9 percent in writing. If this estimate can be used as a valid criterion, the importance of developing listening skills cannot be denied. If children are going to learn to listen effectively, care should be taken to improve upon their auditory perception—the mental interpretation of what a person hears.

Sports activities provide numerous opportunities for the improvement of auditory perception. In games such as football where signals are verbalized, success is dependent upon the auditory clues. Also during participation players receive auditory input from the coach and other players in the form of directions.

The following activities can be used as sports practice drills to sharpen the auditory perception of children.

In the game of *Stoop Tag* the children form a circle and join hands. One child is *It* and stands in the center of the circle. The children walk around the circle saying,

> I am happy, I am free!
> I am down! You can't catch me!

At the word "down," the children stoop and let go of each other's hands. Then they stand up and jump and hop about, daring the child who is *It* to tag them. They must stoop to avoid being tagged. If a child is tagged when not stooping, he becomes *It.* The child first learns to act on the basis of verbal instructions by others. In this regard it has been suggested that later he learns to guide and direct his own behavior on the basis of his own language—he literally talks to himself, giving himself instructions. This point of view has been supported by research which postulates that speech is a form of communication between children and adults that later becomes a means of organizing the child's own behavior. That is, the function which was previously divided between two people—child and adult—later becomes a function of human behavior. The point of this activity is that the child tells himself what to do and then does it. He says, "I am down" and then carries out this action.

In the game of *Dog Chase* the children are divided into five or six groups. The members of each group are given the name of a dog, such as collie, poodle, and so on. The small groups then mingle into one large group. One child, acting as the leader, throws a ball or other object away from the group, at the same time calling out one of the dog names. All of the children with this dog name run after the object. The one who gets possession of it first becomes the leader for the next time. The coach can use this activity as a diagnostic technique by observing those children who react slowly or do not react at all to the auditory input.

In summary, I think it can be seen from the discussions in this chapter that sports, when conducted properly, can contribute much to the intellectual development of children.

Chapter 7

BASIC SPORTS SKILLS FOR CHILDREN

In many cases people make the mistake of labeling a certain condition as luck—good or bad—when in reality the condition is a breakdown in skill performance. Several years ago I conducted a naturalistic observation study of what I termed *sports errors.* In well over 90 percent of the cases these errors were the fault of poor skill performance. A player fumbles a football because he did not have the skill to hold on to the ball, a fielder misses a fly ball because of inability to catch it, and on and on. Thus, coaches should not subscribe to the theory of bad luck when the cause is a lack of or deficiency in skill. It is the major function of this chapter to consider the biomechanics of certain basic movement skills and their importance to successful sports participation for children.

Just as the perception of symbols is concerned with reading readiness, so is basic movement an important factor in readiness to perform in various kinds of sports activities. Since proficient performance in sports activities is dependent upon skill of body movement, the ability of the child to move effectively should be readily discerned.

Skills are the scientific way to move the body and/or its segments in such a way as to expend a minimum amount of energy requirement, but achieve maximum results. Performance of specific skills has been arrived at by scientific insight from such fields as anatomy and kinesiology, which suggests to us how the body can move to achieve maximum efficiency.

Other things being equal, the degree of proficient performance of a skill by any individual is directly related to his or her innate capacity; that is, each individual is endowed with a certain amount of native ability. Through such factors as good teaching, motivation, and the like, attempts are made to help the child perform to the best of his or her particular ability and maintain the highest *skill level.*

FACTORS INVOLVED IN
SKILL TEACHING AND LEARNING

Although each child is born with a certain potential capacity, we should not subscribe to the notion that skills are a part of the child's inheritance. Skills must be learned. In order that a child can participate satisfactorily with his peers, he or she must be given the opportunity to learn the skills under the careful guidance of competent adults.

Perhaps the ideal time to learn certain skills is in childhood. The muscular pliability of the young child is such that there is a desirable setting for the acquisition of various kinds of skills. The child is at a stage in life where there is a great deal of time for practice—a most important factor because children need practice in order to learn—and at this age level they do not seem to become weary of repeating the same thing over and over again. In addition, the young child has a limited number of established skills to obstruct the learning of new skills. Skill learning, therefore, should be facilitated provided competent teaching in the area of sports skills is available.

Experimental research on the influence of specific instruction on various kinds of skills is somewhat limited. More and more scientific evidence is being accumulated, however, which appears to indicate that children in the early elementary school years are mature enough to benefit by instruction in skills such as throwing and jumping.

Following are some suggested guidelines that coaches might take into account in the instruction of skills.

1. The coach should become familiar with the skills involved in a given sports activity. This means that it will be necessary to analyze the activity to determine the extent of the skill requirements.
2. In considering the development of sports skills, the coach should recognize that skills include the following three components: (a) preparing for the movement, (b) executing the movement, and (c) following through. For example, in throwing a ball the individual prepares for the movement by assuming the proper position to throw; he completes the actual throwing of the ball; and finally there is a follow-through action of the arm after the ball leaves the hand. All of these elements are essential to satisfactory performance of this particular skill.

3. The skill should be taught correctly from the beginning; otherwise children may have to do a considerable amount of "unlearning" at a later stage of development.

4. When an error in skill performance is observed, it should be corrected immediately. This can be done under the guidance of the coach by evaluating the child's performance with him or her. Correction of errors in skill performance is essential, first because continued repetition may formulate the faulty practice into a habit, and second because the child will have less difficulty learning more complex skills if he has previously learned easier skills correctly. Coaches should recognize that while there are general patterns for the best performance of skills, individual differences may be considered. This implies that a child should be permitted to deviate from a standard if he or she is able to perform a skill satisfactorily in a manner perculiar to his or her own individual abilities.

5. The greatest amount of time should be spent on skill learning that involves immediate application. In other words, the child should have use for the sports skills being taught so that he can properly apply them commensurate with his stage of development.

6. There is some indication that rhythmic accompaniment is important in the learning of skills. Although the evidence is not definitive and clear-cut, various studies tend to support this contention.

LOCOMOTOR SKILLS

Locomotor skills involve changes in body position that propel the body over the surface area with the impetus being given by the feet and legs. There are five basic types of these skills: walking, running, leaping, jumping, hopping, and three combination skills, which are galloping, skipping, and sliding. The first five of these are performed with an even rhythm, and the last three are done with an uneven rhythm. Locomotor skills require a certain amount of strength and the development of the important sensory-motor mechanisms that are concerned with balance. They also require various degrees of neuromotor coordination for proficient performance.

All of the locomotor skills should be learned correctly by children in the 6–12 year age range. One reason is that these skills comprise the basic requirements for proficiency of performance in the activities contained in a well-planned sports activity program for children. Also, it is important that the child be helped early in life to gain control over the physical aspect of personality, or what is known as *basic body control.*

Coaches and parents should have certain basic knowledge about the locomotor skills so that they will be alert to improve performance of these skills. The following generalized information is intended for this purpose.

Walking

Walking is the child's first experience with bipedal locomotion. He starts to propel himself over the surface area with uneven, full-sole steps (flat-footedness). He is generally referred to as a "toddler," a term that is perhaps derived from the word "tottering." He appears to be tottering to keep in an upright position, which is indicative of the problems he is having with balance and the force of gravity. At about four years of age, on the average, the child's pattern of walking approximates that of an adult.

Ordinarily, when the child is learning to walk, his only teachers are his family members. Because of this, he is not likely to benefit from instruction on correct procedure. As a result, the very important aspect of foot position may be overlooked. Possibly because of this, many children enter school walking in the "toeing out" position rather than pointing the toes straight ahead. Poor walking habits, if allowed to persist, can place an undue amount of strain on certain body parts that in turn may contribute to lack of proficiency in body movement.

Walking involves transferring the weight from one foot to the other. The walk is started with a push-off backward against the surface area with the ball and toes of the foot. After this initial movement the leg swings forward from the hip, the heel of the other foot is placed down, the outer half of the foot next, and the next push-off is made with the toes pointing straight ahead. Of course, walking itself is not an important skill in sports—except in walking races. However, as mentioned, it helps the child improve efficiency in body movement and this is important to some of the other locomotor skills used in sports.

Running

At about 18 months of age, the average child develops a movement that appears to be in between a walk and a run. This is to say that the walking pattern is accelerated, but does not approximate running form. Usually, it is not before ages five or six that the child's running form becomes similar to that used by an adult. As the child gets older he is able to increase his speed of running as well as be able to run greater distances.

Like walking, running involves transferring the weight from one foot to the other, but the rate of speed is increased. The ball of the foot touches the surface area first, and the toes point straight ahead. The body is momentarily suspended in the air when there is no contact with the surface area. This differs from the walk in which contact with either foot is always maintained with the surface area. In the run, there is more flexion at the knee, which involves a higher knee lift. There is also a higher arm lift, with flexion at the elbow reaching a point of about a right angle. In running, there is more of a forward lean than in walking, and in both cases the head points straight ahead. In many instances, the child who has not been taught to run correctly will violate certain mechanical principles by having a backward rather than forward lean, by carrying the arms too high, and by turning the head to the side rather than looking straight ahead.

Running is probably the most used of all the locomotor skills in sports, particularly the team game activities.

Leaping

Leaping, like walking and running, is performed with an even rhythm like a slow run, with one essential difference: the push-off is up and then forward, with the feeling of suspension "up and over." The landing should be on the ball of the foot with sufficient flexion at the knee to absorb the shock. (Incidentally, most sports announcers use the term *leaping* incorrectly. They tend to conceive it as a movement for height, rather than what it really is—a forward locomotor movement. Thus, they refer to some basketball players as "Leapers" when they should be using the term "jumper.")

Although leaping is not used frequently as a specific locomotor skill in many sports activities, there are certain reasons why it is important that children become proficient in this skill. For example, the leap can be combined with the run to leap over an object so as not to deviate from the running pattern. Sometimes this happens with football players leaping over another player on the ground. In addition, in retrieving a ball that has been thrown or hit high, a leap for the ball can help the child catch it "on the run" and thus continue the running pattern, rather than having to stop his movement.

Jumping

In a sense, jumping is somewhat like walking and running in that the movement pattern is similar. However, jumping requires elevation of the body off the surface area, and thus more strength is needed to apply force for this purpose. Usually, the child's first experience with a movement approximating jumping occurs when he steps from a higher to a lower level, as in the case of going down stairs. Although there are many variations in the jumping performance of children, generally speaking, they tend to improve their performance as they get older, with improvement tending to be more pronounced for boys than girls.

Jumping is accomplished by pushing off with both feet and landing on both feet or pushing off with one foot and landing on both feet. Since absorption of shock is important in jumping the landing should be with flexed knees and on the balls of the feet.

Games such as basketball and volleyball require skill in jumping in order to gain success in such activities. The jump becomes a complete activity when children compete against their own performance in individual jumping. This can be done with the standing long jump (taking off and landing on both feet from a standing position) or the running long jump (running to a point and taking off on one foot and landing on both feet). Incidentally the event of high jumping as now performed violates what used to be considered a valid jump. That is, the head was never allowed to go over the bar first. With the advent of the *Fosbury Flop* several years ago, this event could now best be described as a *backward dive*.

Hopping

While hopping is the least difficult of the even rhythmic locomotor skills to describe, at the same time it is perhaps the most difficult to execute. Hopping involves taking off and landing on the same foot. Thus, hopping is a more complex aspect of the jump because the body is elevated from the surface area by the action of only one foot. Not only is greater strength needed for the hop, but also more refined adjustment of balance is required because of the smaller base of support.

Even though hopping is not a specific skill used in most sports activities, one of the more important reasons why children should become proficient in this locomotor skill is that it can help them regain balance in any kind of activity where they have temporarily "lost their footing." When this occurs, the child can use the hop to keep his balance and remain in an upright position while getting the temporarily incapacitated foot into action. Coaches can have children practice this as a drill.

Galloping

The skill of galloping is a combination of the basic pattern of walking and leaping and is performed with an uneven rhythm. Since an uneven rhythmic movement requires more neuromotor coordination, the ability to gallop is developed later than those locomotor movements requiring an even rhythm. The child is likely to learn to gallop before he learns to skip, and about one-half of the children are able to perform at least an approximation of a galloping movement by about the age of four. Between the ages of six and seven most children can perform this movement.

Galloping can be explained by pretending that one foot is injured. A step is taken with the lead foot, but the "injured" foot can bear very little weight and is brought up only behind the other foot and not beyond it. A transfer of weight is made to the lead foot, and thus a fast limp is really a gallop.

Galloping is a skill that does not have prevalent use as a specific skill in most sports activities. One of the most important factors about learning to gallop is that it helps children to be able to change direction in a forward and backward plane more easily. Backward galloping can be done by starting with the lead foot to the back. If a child is proficient in galloping, he will likely be more successful in games that require a forward and/or backward movement for successful performance in that particular activity.

Skipping

Although skipping requires more coordination than galloping, some children will perform variations of the skip around four years of age.

With proper instruction, a majority of children should be able to accomplish this movement by age six.

Skipping can be taught from the walk. A strong push-off should be emphasized. The push-off should be such a forceful upward one that the foot leaves the surface area. In order to maintain balance a hop is taken. The sequence is step, push-off high, hop. The hop occurs on the same foot that was pushing off, and this is the skip. The two actions cause it to be uneven as to rhythm, with a strong or long action (step) and a short one (hop). The reader may recall the mention of skipping in the last chapter as a means of determining kinesthetic sensitivity, and that children could practice it to improve upon this quality.

Sliding

Sliding is much the same as the gallop, but movement is in a sideward direction. One foot is drawn up to the lead foot; weight is shifted from the lead foot to the drawing foot and back again. As in the case of other locomotor skills that are uneven in rhythm, sliding is not used frequently as a specific skill in most sports activities. The important feature of gaining proficiency in the skill of sliding is that it helps the child to be able to change direction skillfully in a lateral plane. Many games involving guarding an opponent, such as basketball, require skill in sliding for success in the game. When a child has developed the skill of sliding from side to side, he does not have to cross his feet and thus can change direction laterally much more easily.

AXIAL SKILLS

Axial skills are nonlocomotor in nature. They can be performed with some parts of the body remaining in contact with the surface area or the body as a whole in gross movement. Included among the axial skills are swinging, bending, stretching, pulling, pushing, and the rotation movements of turning and twisting.

Each of these movements are required at one time or another in the performance of practically all sports activities. Proficiency of performance of the axial skills will improve performance in locomotor skills; for example, the importance of arm swinging in running. When children can perform the axial skills with grace and facility there is a minimum expenditure of energy, and better performance results.

AUXILIARY SKILLS

There are certain skills that are not ordinarily classified as either locomotor or axial. However, they are most important in the successful performance of many sports activities. These skills are arbitrarily identified here as auxiliary skills. Among some of the more important of this type of skill are: starting, stopping, dodging, pivoting, falling, and landing.

Starting

In activities that require responding to a stimulus, such as starting a race, a quick start is an important contribution to success. How well a child will be able to "start" depends upon his reaction time and speed of movement. Reaction time is the amount of time that it takes from the time a signal is given until the onset of the initial movement. Speed of movement is concerned with how fast the person completes the initial movement. Although the factors concerned with starting are innate, they improve with practice. When a coach observes children as being "slow starters," additional help should be given to improve this skill.

Stopping

The skill of stopping is very important because all locomotor movements culminate with this skill. Numerous game activities require quick stopping for successful performance.

Two ways of stopping are the *stride* stop and the *skip* stop. The stride stop involves stopping in running stride. There is flexion at the knees and a slight backward lean to maintain balance. This method of stopping can be used when the performer is moving at a slow speed. The skip stop should be used when there is fast movement, and the performer needs to come to a quick stop. This is accomplished with a hop on either foot, with the other foot making contact with the surface area almost simultaneously. Because of the latter movement, this method of stopping is sometimes called the *jump* stop, because it appears that the performer is landing on both feet at the same time.

Starting and stopping can be practiced in an activity situation with the game *Start and Stop.* In this game, the children are in a straight line with the coach at the goal line some distance away. The coach calls "Start," and on this signal all the children run forward. The coach then calls "Stop," and anyone moving after the signal must return to the starting line. This procedure is continued until one or more children have reached the goal line. The coach should be alert to detect starting and stopping form.

Dodging

Dodging involves changing direction while running. The knees are bent, and the weight is transferred in the dodging direction. This movement is sometimes referred to as "veering" or "weaving." After a dodge is made, the performer can continue in the different direction with a push-off from the surface area with the foot to which the weight was previously transferred. The importance of skill in dodging is seen in games where getting away from an opponent is necessary.

Pivoting

Whereas dodging is used to change direction during body movement, pivoting is employed to change direction while the body is stationary. One foot is kept in contact with the surface area, while the other foot is used to push off. A turn is made in the desired direction with the weight on the foot that has maintained contact with the surface area. The angle of the pivot (turn) is determined by the need in the particular situation. The angle is not likely to be over 180 degrees, as might be the case in pivoting away from an opponent in basketball.

Theoretically, the pivot is executed on only one foot; however, a *reverse turn* is sometimes referred to as a "two-foot" pivot. In this case, a complete turn to the opposite direction is made with both feet on the surface area. With one foot ahead of the other, the heels are raised, and a turn is made with weight equally distributed on both feet.

Pivoting is important in the performance of many kinds of sports activities where quick movements are necessary while the body remains stationary. This is particularly true in games like basketball where a limited number of steps can be taken while in possession of the ball.

Landing

Landing is concerned with the body coming to the surface area from a height or distance. Absorption when landing is accomplished by bending the knees. The weight is on the balls of the feet, and there is flexion at the ankle and knee joints. After landing, the performer comes to an upright position with the arms in a sideward position so as to keep the body in balance.

Many games such as basketball, volleyball, and football require the performer to leave the surface area, which makes the skill of landing important. In addition, vaulting over objects in apparatus activities requires skill in landing, not only for good performance but for safety as well.

Falling

In those activities that require staying in an upright position, emphasis, of course, should be on maintaining this position. Nevertheless, there are occasions when a performer loses balance and falls to the surface area. Whenever possible, a fall should be taken in such a way that injury is least likely to occur. One way to accomplish this is to attempt to "break the fall" with the hands. Relaxation and flexion at the joints that put the performer in a "bunched" position are helpful in avoiding injury when falling to the surface area. Practice of the correct way to make contact with the surface area when falling can take place in connection with the various rolls in gymnastic activities.

SKILLS OF PROPULSION AND RETRIEVAL

Skills which involve propelling and retrieving objects, in most cases a ball, are used in many types of games. It will be the purpose of this section of the chapter to provide the reader with knowledge which is important to an understanding of such propelling and retrieving skills as throwing, striking, kicking, and catching.

Throwing

The skill of throwing involves the release of a ball with one or both hands. In general, there are three factors concerned with success in throwing. These are the accuracy or direction of the throw, the distance in which the ball must be thrown, and the amount of force needed to propel the ball.

Any release of an object from the hand or hands could be considered an act of throwing. Thought of in these terms, the average infant of six months is able to perform a reasonable facsimile of throwing from a sitting position. It has been estimated that by four years of age, about 20% of the children show at least a degree of proficiency in throwing. This ability tends to increase rapidly, and between the ages of five or six, over three-fourths of the children can attain a reasonable degree of proficiency as previously defined here.

Gender differences in the early throwing behavior of children tend to favor boys. At all age levels, boys are generally superior to girls in throwing for distance. There is not such a pronounced gender difference in throwing for accuracy, although the performance of boys in this aspect tends to exceed that of girls.

There are generally three accepted throwing patterns. These are the (1) underarm pattern, (2) sidearm pattern, and (3) overarm pattern. It should be noticed that although the ball is released by one or both hands, the term "arm" is used in connection with the various patterns. The reason is that the patterns involve a "swing" of the arm.

Underarm Throwing Pattern

The child ordinarily begins the underarm throwing pattern by releasing the ball from both hands. However, he is soon able to release with one hand, especially when the ball is small enough to grip.

At the starting position, the thrower stands facing in the direction of the throw. The feet should be in a parallel position and slightly apart. The right arm is in a position nearly perpendicular to the surface area. (All of the descriptions involving the skills of propulsion and retrieval are for the right-handed child. In the case of the left-handed child, just the opposite should apply.) To start the throw, the right arm is brought back (back swing) to a position where it is about parallel with the surface area. Simultaneously, there is a slight rotation of the body to the right with most of the weight transferred to the right foot. As the arm comes forward (front swing) a step is taken with the left foot. (Stepping out with the opposite foot of the swinging arm is known as the *principle of opposition.*) The ball is released on the front swing when the arm is about parallel to the surface area. During the process of the arm swing, the arm is straight, prescribing a semicircle with no flexion at the elbow. The right foot is carried forward as a part of the follow-through after the release.

The underarm throwing pattern is used in games that involve passing the ball from one person to another over a short distance. It is also used for pitching in some baseball-type games.

In their excellent book, *Out of Step,*[1] Dawne Larkin and Debbi Hoare provide some *common and persistent problems* in the performance of some of the propulsion and retrieval skills. I will allude to some of these as appropriate in the discussions to follow. Some of the problems pertaining to the underarm throwing pattern are:

1. Eyes do not focus on the target.
2. Head may be unsteady.
3. Body is not oriented to the target.
4. Throwing arm is not extended sufficiently backwards relative to desired target.
5. Ball release may be inappropriately timed.
6. Ball release may be inefficient because of poor hand and finger control.
7. Follow-through is lacking, or inefficient.
8. Throwing arm may be over extended and trunk forward.
9. Weight may not be transferred forward onto the nonthrowing foot when appropriate.

Sidearm Throwing Pattern

Aside from the direction the thrower faces and the plane of the arm swing, the mechanical principles applied in the sidearm throwing pattern are essentially the same as the underarm throwing pattern.

The thrower faces at a right angle to the direction of the throw, whereas in the underarm throwing pattern he faces in the direction of the throw. The arm is brought to the back swing in a horizontal plane or a position parallel to the surface area. Body rotation and weight shift is the same as in the underarm pattern. The arm remains straight and a semicircle is prescribed from the back swing to the release of the ball on the front swing.

---

[1]Larkin, Dawne and Hoare, Debbi, *Out of Step,* Nedlands, Western Australia, Active Life Foundation, 1991.

The side arm throwing pattern will ordinarily be used to propel a ball that is too large to grip with one hand. Thus, on the back swing the opposite hand helps to control the ball until there is sufficient momentum during the swing. Greater distance can be obtained with the sidearm throwing pattern with a ball too large to grip, but accuracy is more difficult to achieve.

Overarm Throwing Pattern

Again the basic body mechanics of the overarm throwing pattern are essentially the same as the two previous patterns. The thrower faces in the same direction as for the sidearm throwing pattern; that is, at a right angle to the direction of the throw. Depending upon individual differences, this position may vary. An essential difference in the overarm throwing pattern is the position of the arm. Whereas, in the two previous patterns the arm was kept straight, in the overarm throwing pattern there is flexion at the elbow. Thus, on the backswing the arm is brought back with the elbow bent and with the arm at a right angle away from the body. The arm is then brought forward and the ball is released in a "whiplike" motion at about the height of the shoulder. Foot and arm follow through is the same as with the underarm and sidearm throwing patterns. This pattern is used for throwing a ball that can be gripped with the fingers in such games as baseball where distance as well as accuracy are important.

Some common errors in the execution of the overarm throw-pattern are:

1. Eyes may not focus on target.
2. There may be little or no preparatory action.
3. Positioning of wrist or hand with the ball may be incorrect.
4. Base of support may be too wide or too narrow.
5. There may be limited or no rotation of hips and shoulder.
6. The forward rotation of hips, upper trunk and shoulders with arm following may be poorly coordinated.
7. Weight transfer may be nonexistent or inefficient.
8. Not all segments of the arm will contribute to the throw.
9. The forearm may lead the shoulder and elbow.
10. The ball release may be poorly timed.
11. The follow through may be lacking or uncontrolled.
12. The follow through may not be along the flight of the ball.

13. The ball release may be difficult because of poor control of fingers and hand.
14. The nonthrowing arm may not be used to assist throwing.

Striking

Striking involves propelling a ball with a part of the body, ordinarily the hand, as in handball or with an implement such as a bat in baseball. The object to be struck can be stationary; that is, batting a ball from a batting tee or moving such as a pitched ball in baseball.

Some motor development specialists have identified a reasonable facsimile of striking in infancy associated with angry children throwing "nothing" at each other or an adult.

It has long been known that as early as age three, verbal direction to children will educe a sidearm striking pattern with a plastic paddle when a tennis ball is suspended in a stationary position at about waist high. In addition, it has been found that at age three, the child will have a degree of success with the sidearm throwing pattern in striking a light ball when tossed slowly to him.

The principles of body mechanics and the striking patterns are essentially the same as the three previously mentioned throwing patterns— underarm, sidearm, and overarm. The same movements are applied, but in order to propel an object by striking, greater speed is needed with the striking movement. For example, greater speed of movement is needed in the underarm striking pattern when serving a volleyball, than in releasing a ball with a short toss in the underarm throw.

As the child practices striking a ball with a bat from a batting tee, the coach and parent can observe for the following errors in performance:

1. Eyes may not focus on the ball.
2. Base of support may be too narrow or too wide.
3. Stance may be either too far from or too close to the contact point.
4. Lack of weight transference to back foot.
5. Inefficient backwards rotation of hip, spine, shoulders and arms.
6. Weight may not be transferred forward.
7. Arm swing may not be horizontal through ball.
8. Lack of proper follow through.

Kicking

Kicking involves propelling a ball with either foot. As early as age two the average child is able to maintain his balance on one foot and propel a stationary ball with the other foot. At this early age the child is likely to have limited action of the kicking foot with little or no follow through. With advancing age, better balance and strength are maintained that by age six, the child can develop a full leg backswing and a body lean into the kick of a stationary ball.

In kicking, contact with the ball is made with the (1) inside of the foot, (2) outside of the foot, or (3) with the instep of the foot. With the exception of these positions of the foot the mechanical principles of kicking are essentially the same. The kicking leg is swung back with flexion at the knee. The leg swings forward with the foot making contact with the ball. As in the case of the skill of striking, contact with the ball in kicking can be made when the ball is either stationary or moving.

There is not complete agreement in terms of progression in which the skill of kicking is learned. On the basis of personal experience, I recommend the following sequence.

Stationary

The ball and the kicker remain stationary, and the kicker stands beside the ball and kicks it. The kicker is concerned only with the leg movement, and it is more likely that the head will be kept down with the eyes on the ball at the point of contact.

Stationary and Run

This means that the ball is in a stationary position and that the kicker takes a short run up to the ball before kicking it. This is more difficult, as the kicker must time and coordinate the run to make proper contact with the ball.

Kick from Hands

This is referred to as "punting," as in football or soccer. The ball is dropped from the hands of the kicker, and he takes one or two steps and kicks the ball as it drops. He is kicking a moving ball, but he has control over the movement of the ball before kicking it.

Kicking a Moving Ball

Another person could pitch or roll the ball to the kicker as in the game of *kickball.* This is perhaps the most difficult kick because the kicker must kick a moving ball that is or has been under the control of another person, as in the case of the ground ball in soccer.

Catching

In my discussion of visual perception in the last chapter I mentioned about "keeping your eye on the ball" and "looking the ball into your hands." This is concerned with *tracking* which is the ability to maintain focus on a moving object. The importance of tracking in catching should be obvious.

The previously-mentioned Larkin and Hoare point out that tracking patterns vary according to whether the ball is moving through the air or along the ground. It is usually easier to track a moving ball on the ground as more environmental cues are available. The position of the ball in relation to the ground and other objects can be used to help predict its final position. The eyes focus on the ball prior to, and at release to determine the velocity and direction it will travel. The catcher then follows the path intermittently. That is, the eyes do not maintain a steadfast focus on the ball. The catcher should be able to look at the ball and predict its future position in an ongoing manner. This intermittent monitoring allows the processing of other relevant information. This is especially important in many high-skill-level team games where the environment can be unpredictable; that is, movement of other players on the playing area.

Catching with the hands is the most frequently used retrieving skill. One of the child's first experiences with catching occurs at an early stage in life, as when he sits with his legs in a spread position and another person rolls a ball to him. By four years of age, about one-third of the children can retrieve a ball in aerial flight thrown from a short distance. Slightly over one-half can perform this feat by age five, and about two-thirds of them can accomplish this by age six.

There are certain basic mechanical principles that should be taken into account in the skill of catching. It is of importance that the catcher position himself as nearly "in line" with the ball as possible. In this position he will be better able to receive the ball near the center of gravity of the body. Another important factor is hand position. A ball will approach the catcher (1) at the waist, (2) above the waist, or (3) below the waist. When the ball approaches about waist level, the palms should be facing each other with fingers pointing straight ahead. The "heels" of the hands should be close together depending upon the size of the ball; that is, closer for a small ball and farther apart for a large ball. When the ball approaches above the waist, the palms face the ball and the fingers point upward with the thumbs as close together as necessary. When the ball approaches below the waist the palms still face the ball but the fingers face downward with the little fingers as close together as seems necessary. When the ball reaches the hands, it is brought in towards the body; that is, the catcher "gives" with the catch in order to control the ball and absorb the shock. The position of the feet will likely depend upon the speed with which the ball approaches. Ordinarily, one foot should be in advance of the other in a stride position, with the distance determined by the speed of the approaching ball.

The above discussion has been concerned only with retrieving a ball with both hands. Let us examine the skill of catching a ball with one hand.

Most of the research conducted on catching has been that of two-handed catching. An interesting recent study was conducted by Fischman, Moore, and Steele,[2] the primary purpose of which was to begin to describe the development of simple one-hand catching in young children.

The investigation involved 240 children, ranging in age, as of their last birthday, from 5 to 12 years (120 boys and 120 girls). Within each of the eight age groups, 15 boys and 15 girls were observed.

The children were asked to use their preferred hand to catch a total of 24 tennis balls, tossed underarm by an experimenter, from a distance of nine feet. Hand preference was ascertained by asking the children to show which hand they used for brushing their teeth. Of the 240 children, 208 used their right hand and 32 used their left hand.

The nine-foot distance was selected because pilot work indicated that this distance could be used to adequately discriminate between the youngest and oldest children, while proving neither too difficult and frustrating for the 5-year-olds nor too easy for the 12-year-olds. A subject sample was desired that could successfully catch with two hands, espe-

---

[2]Fischman, Mark G., Moore, Jane B., and Steele, Kenneth H., Children's One-Hand Catching as a Function of Age, Gender, and Ball Location, *Research Quarterly for Exercise and Sport,* December 1992.

cially in the younger age groups, and the pilot work showed that a 9-foot distance did produce successful two-hand catching.

Four different locations were designated as the targets for the tosses: (1) Waist height, (2) Shoulder height, (3) Above-the-Head, and (4) Out-to-the-Side, at about waist height. For the first three locations, an attempt was made to place the toss approximately even with the catching arm. For the fourth location, the ball was tossed so that the subjects had to reach out to the side for it but could do so without changing their body position. All balls were tossed at a moderate pace. For the Waist and Out-to-the-Side locations, tosses were made with a slight arc so that the ball was moving downward when the catch was completed. For the Shoulder and Above-the-Head locations, tosses were made so that the ball was still rising when the catch was completed. These trajectories were adjusted slightly to accommodate the subject's height.

Results revealed that catching performance improved with age, boys caught more ball than girls, ball location influenced catching success, and in general, the location of the toss constrained the child's selection of an appropriate hand-arm orientation. With the possible exception of the Shoulder location for girls, even very young children are sensitive to the perceptual aspects of the toss and respond with an appropriate orientation.

There are few instances where a child uses the one-hand catch in sports activities. An exception, of course, is in baseball, but the catch is made easier with the use of a glove.

SKILLS AS SPECIFIC SPORTS EVENTS

Sometimes contests of skill become single sports events. For example, basketball freethrowing, throwing a ball for accuracy, and throwing for distance.

Over the years the *Punt, Pass & Kick* (PP&K) contest has been one of the most popular of these. This contest started on a national level in the mid 1960s with children in the 8–13 year age range competing against each other at the same age level in punting, passing, and kicking a football. Contests were held at district, regional, and finally at the national level during the half of the Super Bowl. In 1980 the program was curtailed; however, in 1992 it was restored with the National Football League (NFL) encouraging girls to participate as well as boys. Over 300,000 children participated in 1,600 local programs.

The program was actually revived in 1991 when the NFL decided to test-market it in five cities. When so many children signed up to participate the league was able to get Gatorade to be the sponsor. The competition which began again in September 1992 involved all 28 of the NFL teams.

Many present NFL stars participated as children in the program, including Dan Marino, Miami; Randall Cunningham, Philadelphia; Bernie Kosar, Cleveland; and Jim Kelly, Buffalo. Kelly has been quoted as saying, "I was so happy to see it come back. I honestly believe it's the main reason I am where I am. It made me work at football. My ultimate goal was to be a quarterback in the NFL, and I started practicing for PP&K when I was six years old."[3]

Scores in the PP&K are based on distance and accuracy. That is, if a participant throws the football 100 feet but it lands 20 feet to the left of the measuring tape the total score is 100 minus 20 for a score of 80. A participant receives one punt, one pass, and one kick. The distances are added together for the final total score.

In closing this chapter, I want to state that it should be obvious that how well a child is able to perform certain basic skills is directly related to the success he or she will have in a sport requiring those skills. For this reason care should be taken to see that children are well prepared in skill performance. To a large extent this ability will be a factor in the type of sports a child will be able to engage in successfully. Unfortunately, some children are pressured into certain sports by parents at too early an age before the child is ready for the skill levels required in those sports.

---

[3]Shapiro, Leonard, Again, PP&K Starts Ball Rolling, *The Washington Post,* December 17, 1992.

Chapter 8

THE COACH OR PARENT AS A
TEACHER OF SPORTS ACTIVITIES

As nearly as I have been able to determine, the earliest use of the term *coach* occurred somewhere around mid 19th century. It was used in Great Britain to describe a tutor who conveyed a student through his examinations. It soon found use in this country and was considered as one who instructs players in the fundamentals of competitive sports and directs team strategy.

Although it is not always the case, a coach should first and foremost be a teacher. This being the case, there are certain concepts and understandings that coaches should have about teaching.

The term *teacher* in the present discussion refers to coaches, parents, or other adults who have the responsibility for teaching children about sports. Although it is the coach who will probably have the major responsibility, it is important that interested parents also have some knowledge of valid teaching procedures.

The qualified teacher is aware that every child is almost incredibly unique and that he or she approaches all learning tasks with his or her own level of motivation, capacity, experience, and vitality. Moreover, such a teacher is aware that the individual in a group must be prepared for a learning experience so that the experience may, in some way, be recognized as having meaning. Preparation of any team must be in terms of the particular individuals on that team. The teacher must then, by a combination of emotional and logical appeal, help each individual find his or her way through the experience at his or her own rate and, to some extent, in his or her own way. The teacher must also help the individual "nail down" the meaning of the experience to himself or herself and help to incorporate it and its use into his or her own life. The point of view reflected here is that there is no substitute for a competent teacher who, while necessarily teaching a group, is highly sensitive to the individual children involved.

119

The teacher's role should be that of a guide who supervises and directs desirable sports learning experiences. In providing such experiences, the teacher should constantly keep in mind how sports can contribute to the previously-mentioned physical, social, emotional, and intellectual development of every child. This implies that the teacher should develop an understanding of principles of learning and to apply these principles properly in the teaching of sports activities. (These principles will be discussed in detail later in the chapter.)

It is important that the teacher recognize that individual differences exist among teachers as well as children and that some of these differences will influence their teaching methods. Sometimes one teacher may have greater success than another with a method. This implies that there should be no specified resolute method of teaching for all teachers. On the other hand, teachers should allow themselves to deviate from recommended conformity if they are able to provide desirable learning experiences through a method peculiar to their own abilities. This, of course, means that the procedures used should be compatible with conditions under which learning takes place best.

CHARACTERISTICS OF GOOD TEACHERS

Over the years there have been numerous attempts to identify objectively those characteristics of good teachers that set them apart from average or poor teachers. Obviously, this is a difficult matter because of the countless variables involved.

It is entirely possible for two teachers to possess the same degree of intelligence, preparation, and understanding of what they are teaching. Yet, it is also possible that one of these teachers will consistently achieve good results with children, while the other will not have much success. Perhaps a good part of the reason for this difference in success lies in those individual differences of teachers that relate to certain personality factors and how they deal and interact with children. Based upon the available research and numerous interviews with both teachers and children, I have found the following characteristics tend to emerge most often among good teachers.

1. Good teachers possess those characteristics that in one way or another have a humanizing effect on children. An important factor of good teachers that appeals to most children is a sense of humor. One

10-year-old boy put it this way, "She laughed when we played a joke on her."

2. In all cases, good teachers are fair and democratic in their dealings with children and tend to maintain the same positive feelings toward the so-called "problem" child as they do with other children.

3. Another very important characteristic is that good teachers are able to relate easily to children. They have the ability and sensitivity to "listen through children's ears and see through children's eyes."

4. Good teachers are flexible. They know that different approaches need to be used with different groups of children as well as individual children. In addition, good teachers can adjust easily to changing situations.

5. Good teachers are creative. This is an extremely important factor, because in sports experiences with children they are dealing with a very imaginative segment of the population.

6. Good teachers have control. Different teachers exercise control in different ways, but good teachers tend to have a minimum of control problems probably because they provide a learning environment where control becomes a minimum problem.

TEACHING AND LEARNING IN SPORTS

The teaching-learning process is complicated and complex. For this reason it is important that teachers have as full an understanding as possible of the role of teaching and learning in sports.

Basic Considerations

The concepts of learning that a teacher subscribes to are directly related to the kind and variety of sports learning experience and activities that will be provided for children. For this reason it is important for teachers to explore some of the factors that make for the most desirable and worthwhile learning. Among the factors that should help to orient the reader with regard to some basic understandings in the teaching of sports activities are (1) an understanding of the meaning of certain terms, (2) an understanding of the derivation of teaching methods, and (3) an understanding of the various learning products in sports.

Meaning of Terms

Due to the fact that certain terms, because of their multiple use, do not actually have a universal definition, no attempt will be made here to define terms. On the other hand, it will be the purpose to describe certain terms rather than attempt to define them. The reader should view the descriptions of terms that follow with this general idea in mind.

Learning. Without exception, most definitions of learning are characterized by the idea that learning involves some sort of change in the individual. This means that when an individual has learned, behavior is modified in one or more ways. Thus, a valid criterion for learning would be that after having an experience, a person could behave in a way in which he could not have behaved before having had the experience. In this general connection, many learning theorists suggest that it is not possible to "see" learning. However, behavior can be seen, and when a change in behavior has occurred, then it is possible to infer that change and learning have occurred. Figure 5 depicts this concept.

LEARNING CAN BE INFERRED BY A CHANGE IN BEHAVIOR

Children behave in a given way	$\rightarrow$	Children are in the teaching-learning situation	$\rightarrow$	Children behave in a way that is different than before they were in the teaching-learning situation

Figure 5.

Teaching. Several years ago I was addressing a group of teachers on the subject of teaching and learning. Introducing the discussion in somewhat abstract terms, I asked, "What is teaching?" After a short period of embarrassing deliberation, one member of the group interrogated the following answer with some degree of uncertainty: "Is it imparting information?" This kind of thinking is characteristic of that which reflects the traditional meaning of the term "teaching." A more acceptable description of teaching would be to think of it in terms of guidance, direction, and supervision of behavior that results in desirable and worthwhile learning. This is to say that it is the job of the teacher to guide the child's learning rather than to impart to him a series of unrelated and sometimes meaningless facts.

Method. The term "method" might be considered as an orderly and systematic means of achieving an objective. In other words, method is concerned with "how to do" something in order to achieve desired results. If best results are to be obtained for children in their sports experiences, it becomes necessary that the most desirable sports learning experiences be provided. Consequently, it becomes essential that teachers use all of the ingenuity and resourcefulness at their command in the proper direction and guidance of these learning experiences. The procedures that teachers use are known as *teaching methods.*

Derivation of Teaching Methods

Beginning teachers often ask, "Where do we get our ideas for teaching methods?" For the most part this question should be considered in general terms. In other words, although there are a variety of acceptable teaching procedures, all of these methods are likely to be derived from two somewhat broad sources.

The first of these involves an accumulation of knowledge of educational psychology and what is known about the learning process in providing sports learning experiences. The other is the practice of successful teachers.

In most instances, preparation of prospective teachers includes at least some study of educational psychology as it applies to the learning process and certain accepted principles of learning. With this basic information it is expected that beginning teachers have sufficient knowledge to make application of it in the practical situation. (Unfortunately, many children's coaches will not have had this preparation.)

It has been my observation over a period of years that many beginning teachers tend to rely too much upon the practices of successful teachers as a source of teaching methods. The validity of this procedure is based on the assumption that such successful practices are likely to have as their bases the application of fundamental psychological principles of learning. Nevertheless, it should be the responsibility of every teacher to become familiar with the basic psychological principles of learning and to attempt to apply these in the best possible way when providing the most desirable and worthwhile sports learning experiences for children.

Learning Products of Sports

In general, three learning products can be identified that accrue from participation in sports activities, namely, direct, incidental, and indirect. In a well-planned program, these learning products should develop satisfactorily through sports activities.

Direct learning products are those that are the direct object of teaching. For instance, running, dodging, throwing, and catching are some of the important skills necessary for reasonable degrees of proficiency in the game of basketball. Through the learning of skills, more enjoyment is derived from participating in an activity than just the practice of the skills. For this reason, the learning of skills is one of the primary direct objects of teaching. However, it should be understood that certain incidental and indirect learning products can result from direct teaching in sports. The zeal of a participant to become a more proficient performer gives rise to certain incidental learning products. These may be inherent in the realization and acceptance of practices of healthful living, which make the individual a more skilled performer in the activity.

Attitudes have often been considered in terms of behavior tendencies and as such might well be concerned with indirect learning products. This type of learning product involves such qualities as sportsmanship, appreciation of certain aspects of the activity, and other factors that involve the adjustment and modification of the individual's reaction to others.

Adults who have the responsibility for providing sports programs for children should give a great deal of consideration to these various kinds of learning products. This is particularly important if children are to receive the full benefit of sports learning experiences that are provided for them.

SOME PRINCIPLES OF LEARNING APPLIED TO SPORTS

There are various basic facts about the nature of human beings of which we are more cognizant than we were in the past. Essentially, these facts involve some of the fundamental aspects of the learning process, which all good teaching should take into account. Older concepts of teaching methods were based largely on the idea that the teacher was the sole authority in terms of what was best for children, and that children were expected to learn regardless of the conditions surrounding the learning situation. For the most part, modern teaching replaces the older concepts with methods that are based on certain accepted belief of educational psychology. Outgrowths of these beliefs emerge in the form of principles of learning. The following principles provide important guidelines for arranging learning experiences for children, and they suggest how desirable learning can take place when the principles are satisfactorily applied to sports.

1. *The Child's Own Purposeful Goals Should Guide His Learning Activities.* In order for a desirable learning situation to prevail, teachers must consider certain features about purposeful goals which guide learning activities. Of utmost importance is the fact that the goal must seem worthwhile to the child. This will perhaps involve such factors as interest, attention, and motivation. Fortunately, in sports activities such factors as interest, attention, and motivation are likely to be inherent qualities. Thus, the teacher does not always necessarily need to "arouse" the child with various kinds of motivating devices.

The goal should not be too difficult for the child to achieve. While it should present a challenge, it should be something that is commensurate with the child's abilities and within the realm of achievement. By the same token, the goal should not be too easy or it will not be likely that the child will have the opportunity to develop to his or her greatest capacity. To be purposeful, a goal should give direction to activity and learning. In substance, this implies that after a child has accepted a goal he should have a better idea of where he is going and what he should be able to accomplish in a given situation.

It is important that the child find, adopt, and accept his or her own goals. This implies that the child should not receive them directly from the teacher. If the most desirable learning is to take place, it is doubtful if one person can give another person a goal. This should not be interpreted to mean that goals should not originate with the teacher. On the contrary, the teacher can be of considerable help in assisting children to find their own goals. This can be done by planning the sports learning environment in such a way that children with varying interests and abilities may find something that appears worthwhile.

2. *The Child Should Be Given Sufficient Freedom to Create His Own Responses in the Situation He Faces.* This principle indicates that *problem solving* is a very important way of human learning and that the child will learn largely only through experience, either direct or indirect. This

implies that the teacher should provide every opportunity for children to utilize judgment in the various situations that arise in sports.

It should be borne in mind that although the child learns through experience, this does not mean that experience will assure desirable learning, since it might possibly come too soon. For example, it is doubtful that children at the first-grade level should be expected to learn some of the complex skill patterns in the highly organized game of football, simply because at that level they are not likely to be ready for it.

When children are free to create their own responses in the situation they face, individual differences are being taken into consideration, and, generally, experience comes at the right time for desirable learning. This situation necessitates an activity area environment flexible to the extent that children can achieve in relation to their individual abilities.

In a sense, this principle of learning refutes, and perhaps rightly so, the idea that there is a specific "problem-solving method" mutually exclusive from other methods. In other words, all methods should involve some aspect of problem solving, which actually means the application of this principle.

3. *The Child Agrees to and Acts Upon the Learnings Which He Considers of Most Value to Him.* Children accept as most valuable those things which are of greatest interest to them. This principle implies in part, then, that there should be a satisfactory balance between *needs* and *interests* of children as criteria for the selection of sports activities. Although it is of extreme importance to consider the needs of children in developing experiences, the teacher should not lose sight of the fact that their interest is needed if the most desirable learning is to take place.

While needs and interests of children may be closely related, there are nevertheless differences that should be taken into consideration when sports learning activities are selected. Interests are mostly acquired as products of the environment, while needs, particular those of an individual nature, are more likely to be innate. Herein lies one of the main differences in the two criteria insomuch as the selection of sports learning activities are implicated. For instance, a child may demonstrate a temporary interest in an activity that may not contribute to his needs at a certain age level. This interest may be aroused because of the child's environment. Perhaps an older brother, sister or a parent may influence a child to develop an interest in an activity that would not contribute to his needs or possibly have a detrimental effect on him. Despite the inevitability of such contingencies, interests of children may serve as one of the valid criteria for the selection of sports learning activities.

To a certain extent interests may be dependent upon past experiences of children. For instance, interests in certain sports may stem from the fact that they are a part of the traditional background of the community and as such have absorbed the interest of parents as well as children.

4. ***The Child Should Be Given the Opportunity to Share Cooperatively in Learning Experiences with Teammates Under the Guidance, But Not the Control of the Teacher.*** The point that should be emphasized here is that although learning may be an individual matter, it is likely to take place best in a group. This is to say that children learn individually, but that socialization should be retained. Moreover, sharing in group activities seems absolutely essential in educating for democracy.

The sports situation should present near-ideal conditions for a desirable balance between individualization and socialization. For example, the elements of an activity must be learned individually, but then they are combined by the entire team in a game situation. In a game, each child learns how to perform the skills necessary for successful performance in the game situation. However, he may improve his skills or application of skill when he is placed in the actual game situation. Another example may be seen in the performance of certain gymnastic activities. Although these are predominantly individual in nature, children oftentimes work together in small groups assisting each other and, as a consequence, are likely to learn from each other by pooling and sharing experience.

5. ***The Teacher Should Act as a Guide Who Understands the Child as a Growing Organism.*** This principle indicates that the teacher should consider learning as an evolving process and not just as instantaneous behavior. If teaching is to be regarded as the guidance and direction of behavior which results in learning, the teacher must display wisdom as to when to "step in and teach" and when to step aside and watch for further opportunities to guide and direct behavior.

The application of this principle precludes an approach of teacher domination. On the other hand, the implementation of this principle is perhaps more likely to be realized in sports where the teacher recognizes that numerous problem-solving situations are inherent in many sports situations. For example, if a practice session is not going as it should, the teacher can stop the activity and evaluate it with the children so that they can determine how the activity may be improved. In other words, children are placed in a position to identify problems connected with the activity and given the opportunity to exercise judgment in solving them. The teacher thus helps the children discover direct pathways to meaningful areas of experience and at the same time contributes to the children's ability to become self-directed individuals.

PHASES OF THE TEACHING–LEARNING SITUATION

There are certain fundamental phases involved in almost every sports teaching-learning situation. These are (1) auditory input, (2) visual input, (3) participation, and (4) evaluation. Although these four phases are likely to be weighted in various degrees, they will occur in the teaching of practically every sports situation regardless of the type of activity that is being taught. While the application of the various phases may be of a general nature, they nevertheless should be utilized in such a way that they become specific in a particular situation. Depending upon the type of activity being taught, the use and application of the various phases should be characterized by flexibility and awareness of the objectives of the situation.

Auditory-Input Phase

As mentioned previously, the term *auditory* may be described as stimulation occurring through the sense organs of hearing. The term *input* is concerned with the use of as many media as are deemed necessary for a particular teaching-learning situation. The term *output* is concerned with behaviors or reactions of the learner resulting from the various forms of input. Auditory input involves the various learning media that are directed to the auditory sense. This should not be interpreted to mean that the auditory-input phase of the teaching-learning situation is a one-way process. While much of such input may originate with the teacher, consideration should also be given to the verbal interaction among children and between the children and the teacher.

Sports provide a most desirable opportunity for learning through direct, purposeful experience. In other words, the sports learning situation is "learning by doing," or learning through pleasurable physical activity. Although verbalization might well be kept to a minimum, a certain amount of auditory input, which should provide for auditory-motor association, appears to be essential for a satisfactory teaching-learning situation. The quality of "kinesthetic feel" may be described as the process of changing ideas into muscular action and is of primary importance in the proper acquisition of sports skills. It might be said that the auditory-input phase of teaching helps to set the stage for a kinesthetic concept of the particular activity being taught.

Great care should be taken with the auditory-input phase in sports teaching-learning situations. The ensuing discussions are intended to suggest to the reader ways in which the greatest benefits can accrue when using this particular learning medium.

Preparing the Children for Listening

Since it is likely that the initial part of the auditory-input phase will originate with the teacher, care should be taken to prepare the children for listening. The teacher may set the scene for listening by relating the activity to the interests of children. In addition, the teacher should be on the alert to help children develop their own purposes for listening.

In preparing children to listen, the teacher should be aware that it is of importance that the comfort of the children be taken into consideration and that attempts should be made for removing any possible attention-distracting factors. Although evidence concerning the effect of environmental distractions on listening effectiveness is not in great abundance, there is reason to believe that distraction does interfere with listening comprehension. Moreover, it was reported years ago that being able to see as well as hear the speaker is an important factor in listening distraction.

These factors have a variety of implications for the auditory-input phase of the sports teaching-learning-situation. For example, consideration should be given to the placement of children when a sports activity requires auditory input by the teacher. This means, for instance, that if the teacher is providing auditory input from a circle formation, the teacher should take a position as part of the circle instead of speaking from the center of the circle. Also, it might be well for teachers to consider that an object, such as a ball, can become an attention-distracting factor when an activity is being discussed. The attention of the children is sometimes focused on the ball, and they may not listen to what is being said. The teacher might wish to conceal such an object until time for its use is most appropriate.

Teacher-Child and Child-Child Interaction

It was mentioned previously that the auditory-input phase is a two-way process. As such, it is important to take into account certain factors involving verbal interaction of children with children, and teacher with children.

By "democracy" some people seem to mean everyone doing or saying whatever happens to cross his mind at the moment. This raises the question of control, and it should be emphasized that group discussions, if they are to be democratic, must be in control. This is to say that if a group discussion is to succeed it must be under control, and let me stress that democracy implies discipline and control.

Group discussion is a kind of sociointellectual exercise (involving numerous bodily movements, of course) just as basketball is a kind of sociointellectual exercise (involving, too, higher mental functioning). Both imply individual discipline to keep play moving within bounds, and both require moderators, (or officials) overseeing, though not participating in, the play in the manner that is objective and aloof from the heat of competition. In brief, disciplined, controlled group discussion can be a training ground for living in a society in which both individual and group interests are profoundly respected—just as games can serve a comparable function.

Another important function in teacher-child verbal interaction is with the time given to questions after the teacher has provided auditory input. The teacher should give time for questions from the group, but should be very skillful in the use of questions. It must be determined immediately whether or not a question is a legitimate one. This implies that the type of questions asked can help to serve as criteria for the teacher to evaluate the auditory-input phase of teaching. For example, if numerous questions are asked, it is apparent that either the auditory input from the teacher was unsatisfactory or the children were not paying attention.

Directionality of Sound

In summarizing recent findings concerned with the directionality of sound, a number of interesting factors important to the auditory-input phase have emerged. For example, individuals tend to initiate movements toward the direction from which the sound cue emanates. That is, if a verbal cue is given that instructs the individual to move a body segment or segments to the left, but the verbal cue emanates from the right side of the individual, the initial motor response is to the right, followed by a reverse response to the left. It is recommended that when working on direction of motor responses with children, one should make certain that sound cues come from the direction in which the motor response is made. The point is that children have enough difficulty in discriminating left from right without confusing them further.

Visual-Input Phase

Various estimates indicate that the visual sense brings us upwards of three-fourths of our knowledge. If this postulation can be used as a valid criterion, the merits of the visual-input phase in teaching about sports are readily discernible. In many cases, visual input, which should provide for visual-motor association, serves as a happy medium between verbal symbols and direct participation in helping teachers further prepare children for the kinesthetic feel mentioned previously.

In general, there are two types of visual input which can be used satisfactorily in teaching about sports. These are visual symbols and human demonstration (live performance).

Visual Symbols

Included among the visual symbols used in sports are motion pictures and various kinds of flat or still pictures. One of the disadvantages of the latter centers around the difficulty in portraying movement with a still figure. Although movement is obtained with a motion picture, it is not depicted in third dimension, which causes some degree of ineffectiveness when this medium is used. One valuable use of visual symbols is that of employing diagrams to show the dimensions of activity areas.

Human Demonstration

Some of the guides to action in the use of demonstration follow:

1. If the teacher plans to demonstrate, this should be included in the preparation by practicing and rehearsing the demonstration.
2. The teacher does not need to do all of the demonstrating; in fact, in some cases it may be much more effective to have one or more children demonstrate. Since the teacher is expected to be a skilled performer, a demonstration by a child will oftentimes serve to show

other children that one of their peers can perform the activity and that they should be able to do it also.

3. A demonstration should be based on the skill and ability of a given group of children. If it appears to be too difficult for them, they might not want to attempt the activity.

4. When at all possible, a demonstration should parallel the timing and conditions of when it will be put to practical application. However, if the situation is one in which the movements are complex or done with great speed, it might be well to have the demonstration conducted on a slower basis than that involved in the actual performance situation.

5. The group should be arranged so that everyone is in a favorable position to see the demonstration. Moreover, the children should be able to view the demonstration from a position where it takes place. For example, if the activity is to be performed in a lateral plane, children should be placed so that they can see it from this position.

6. Although auditory input and human demonstration can be satisfactorily combined in many situations, care should be taken that auditory input is not lost, because the visual sense offsets the auditory sense; that is, one should not become an attention-distracting factor for the other. It will be up to the teacher to determine the amount of verbalization that should accompany the demonstration.

7. After the demonstration has been presented it may be a good practice to demonstrate again and have the children go through the movements with the demonstrator. This provides for use of the kinesthetic sense together with the visual sense that makes for close integration of these two sensory stimuli.

Participation Phase

The following considerations should be kept in mind in connection with the participation phase of teaching.

1. The practice session should be planned so that the greatest possible amount of time is given to participation.

2. If the activity does not progress as expected in the participation phase, perhaps the fault may lie in the procedures used in the auditory- and visual-input phases. Participation then becomes a criterion for the evaluation of former phases.

3. The teacher should take into account the fact that the original attempts in learning an activity should meet with a reasonable degree of success.

4. The teacher should constantly be aware of the possibility of fatigue of children during participation and should understand that individual differences in children create a variation with regard to how rapidly fatigue takes place.

5. Participation should be worthwhile for every child, and all children should have the opportunity to achieve.

6. The teacher should be ever on the alert to guide and direct learning, thus making the practice session a good teaching-learning experience.

7. During the participation phase, the teacher should constantly analyze the performance of children in order to determine those who need improvement in skills. Behaviorisms of children should be observed while they are engaging in the sports activity. For example various types of emotional behavior might be noted in sports situations that might not be indicated in any other experience.

8. Problems involved during participation should be kept in mind for subsequent evaluation with the children.

Evaluation Phase

Evaluation is a very important phase of the sports teaching-learning situation, and yet, perhaps one of the most neglected aspects of it. For instance, it is not an uncommon procedure to have a practice session end at a signal, with the children hurrying and scurrying from the activity area without an evaluation of the results of the session.

Children should be given the opportunity to discuss the session and to suggest ways in which improvement might be effected. When this procedure is followed, children are placed in a problem-solving situation and desirable learning is more likely, with the teacher guiding learning rather than dominating the situation in a direction-giving type of procedure. Also more and better continuity is likely to be provided from one session to another when time is taken for evaluation. In addition, children are much more likely to develop a clearer understanding of the purposes of sports if they are given an opportunity to discuss the procedures involved.

Ordinarily, the evaluation phase should take place at the end of the session. Experience has shown that a satisfactory evaluation procedure can be effected in six to eight minutes, depending upon the nature of the activity and upon what actually occurred during the session. Under certain circumstances, if an activity is not proceeding well in the participation phase, it may be desirable to stop the activity and carry out what is known as a "spot" evaluation. This does not mean that the teacher should stop an activity every time the situation is not developing according to plan. A suggestion or a hint to children who are having difficulty with performance can perhaps preclude the need for having all of the children cease participation. On the other hand, if the situation is such that the needs of the group will best be met by a discussion concerning the solution of a problem, the teacher is indeed justified in stopping the activity and conducting an evaluation "on the spot."

In concluding this chapter, let me say that if the teacher is to provide sports learning experiences that contribute to total development of children, there must be a clear perspective of the total learning that is expected from the area of sports. This implies that in order to provide for progression in sports learning there must be some means of preserving continuity from one practice session to another. Consequently, each individual session becomes a link in the chain of sports learnings that contributes to the total development of the child. Experience has shown that the implementation of this theory into reality can be most successfully accomplished by wise and careful planning of practice sessions.

Chapter 9

FOOTBALL AND SOCCER

Football and soccer are the two games where players literally "put their foot in it." This moreso in soccer than in football.

The foot is used in football with three types of kicks: punt, placekick and kickoff. In the punt the ball is dropped from the hands and kicked and in the placekick the ball is held on the ground by a holder with a stationary kick and run. It is the same for the kickoff but the ball is kicked from a tee. The placekick is used for extra points after touchdowns and for field goals. The kickoff is used to start the game or to kick to the team that has just been scored on.

During the early history of the game and through the 1920s, the dropkick was used pretty much for extra points and field goals. The ball is dropped to the ground and kicked when it makes impact with the ground. As rule changes made the ball more oval shaped, the dropkick became almost extinct because more accuracy could be obtained with the placekick.

In most football games there is a minimum of kicking because most of the time is spent on running or passing the ball.

On the other hand, the game of soccer uses the feet and legs almost exclusively. Compared to football, in soccer the use of the feet and legs for playing the ball reduces the complexity of movement options that the child will have to deal with. The arms are free to enhance balance. This is a very good activity for children who have fine control problems with the upper limbs or hands. Soccer allows children with this type of movement dysfunction to work within the range of their abilities and circumvent their disability.[1]

---

[1]Larkin, Dawne and Hoare, Debbi, *Out of Step,* Nedlands, Western Australia, Active Life Foundation, 1991.

FOOTBALL

In the United States the word *football* generally refers only to the
American game; in other parts of the world it usually means soccer. Most
of the modern forms of football are derived from many ancient games,
especially *harpaston* and *harpastrum,* played in Greece and Rome. These
games were carried over through the Middle Ages down to present times
in Tuscany and Florence under the name of *calcio.* Meanwhile a rugged
undisciplined type of football took root in England in the Middle Ages,
and despite several edicts banning the game from time to time, football
remained popular among the masses until the early 19th century. Different forms of the game were soon developed at the various English public
schools—Rugby, Eton, Harrow, and others. Eventually two main games
emerged. One was primarily a kicking game, which later became association football, or soccer; the other (dating from 1823) was football as
played at Rugby, in which carrying the ball and tackling were permitted.
It was from the two English games, especially rugby, that American
football developed.[2]

The American game is played by two opposing teams of 11 players
each. (In some high schools with a small enrollment, a team consists of
six players.) The field is level and is 100 yards long and 53⅓ yards wide.
It is marked off by latitudinal stripes every five yards and is flanked on
each end by an endzone 10 yards deep. In each endzone stand H-shaped
goal posts not exceeding 20 feet in height, with the crossbar 10 feet from
the ground and with the vertical posts 24 feet apart. (The dimensions
of the playing field may be modified for younger players.) Play is
directed toward gaining possession of the football—an inflated egg-
shaped leather ball—and moving it across the opponent's goal line,
thereby scoring a touchdown, worth six points. In advancing the ball a
team may run or pass (forward or laterally), but it must gain 10 yards in
four tries (or downs), or else yield possession of the ball to the opponent.
The defending team tries to stop the ball carrier from advancing by
tackling him; that is, forcing him to the ground—thus causing the team
with ball to use up one of its downs. The defending team can gain
possession of the ball before the end of four downs by recovering a
dropped ball (fumble), or by intercepting a pass. Because of the strategies and skills required, most organized football clubs have offensive and

---

[2]*The New Columbia Encyclopedia,* New York, Columbia University Press, fourth edition, 1975, Eds.
William H. Harris and Judith S. Levy.

defensive squads that alternate on the field as possession of the ball changes.

In addition to the touchdown, points are scored by kicking the ball over the crossbar between the goal posts (field goal) counting three points; and by downing a player in possession of the ball behind his own goal line (a safety), counting two points. Additional points, known as conversions (extra points), may be scored after completion of a touchdown. In professional play the conversion is worth one point and is earned by kicking the ball over the crossbar of the goal post or by running or passing the ball over the goal line from two yards away. In amateur (high school and college) football, where the conversion play is begun three yards away from the goal line, the kick is worth one point and the running or passing conversion, two points. When a team is not likely to gain 10 yards in four downs, it often kicks, or punts the ball downfield, usually on the fourth down. After each down before resuming play, the opposing teams face each other along an imaginary line of scrimmage, determined by the position of the ball relative to the goals.

Blocking and tackling make football one of the most rugged sports played; thus, football players wear heavy protective gear. (This is a reason often given by many parents for not permitting their children to play the game.)

Although participation in football (particularly "tackle" football) by children is a controversial issue among some parents, it is a popular sport among many children. In my surveys football rated high among boys in sports they "liked to play best." Also, there appears to be an increasing interest in the game among girls—particularly the football type games that do not involve tackling.

Some programs appear to be carried out with much success. For example, in Prince George's County, Maryland, 30 of 32 Boys and Girls Clubs sponsor 160 teams for children and youth ages 7 to 16 and weighing 70 to 150 pounds. These teams have wide support of parents whose children participate.

According to my interviews with parents, coaches, professional players, and children themselves, there is little or no agreement on the age at which children should be allowed to participate in the "tackle" version of football. One school of thought is reflected in the belief of one coach who has coached Boys Club 8–9-year-olds for seven years. His feeling is that at that age level they are not "big enough or strong enough to knock each other around." He maintained that in his seven-year tenure there were no serious injuries incurred by his or opposing players.

Conversely, many professional football players seem to prefer that their own children wait to participate until they are at least of high school age. The reason given by many of these professionals is essentially the same as that of most educators who feel that the contact in football can be harmful to the development of growing children. In fact, a quarterback who has played in the National Football League for 10 years indicated that he had to "fight off" his own son's participation until he was 13 years of age. He said that he was forced to relent because of his child's loss of status among his peers.

Some persons feel that children will play football on their own anyway so their thinking is "why not be organized with proper equipment if appropriate supervision is provided."

There is no question about it; this is not an easy problem for a parent to resolve. As I have stated previously, parents should thoroughly explore the type of supervision that will be available to assure the safety and well being of the child who prefers to participate. Parents should resist the temptation to relive their own lives through their children—particularly those fathers who were themselves, "frustrated athletes." Moreover, it is doubtful that there is any reason why a child should be *pressured* into participating in any sport if he or she desires not to do so.

FOOTBALL SKILLS

There are a number of skills that need to be acquired if one is to have success in football.

Passing

An important thing to remember in football skills is the shape of the ball. In all other games the ball is round. And, of course, the balls come in different sizes as we can see when we compare a basketball and a baseball. Because the ball is oval shaped in football some of the skills may be more difficult to perform. There are two kinds of passes in football, the *forward* pass, and the *lateral* pass.

Forward Pass

The first thing to think about in forward passing is how to grip the ball. The fingers of the throwing hand grip the lace behind the center of the ball. The fingers are spread over the laces and the thumb around the ball. The smaller the hand, the nearer the end of the ball it should be.

The pass is made with the overarm throwing pattern which was explained in Chapter 7. A right-handed thrower can use the left hand to help hold the ball while gripping it with the right hand. The ball is brought back past the ear. The body turns a little away from the direction of the throw. There is a step forward with the left foot pointing in the direction of the target. The weight shifts from the right foot to the left foot. The elbow of the throwing arm moves forward. The forearm comes forward with a whipping action with the ball rolling off the finger tips. The ball should be thrown a little ahead of the person who is to catch it. This is the receiver who will be moving. Here are some important things to remember when throwing a forward pass.

1. Be sure to point the left foot in the direction of the throw if right-handed. If left-handed, the right foot will be pointed in the direction of the throw.
2. Grip the ball where it is most comfortable. The thrower may have to grip it nearer the end if he has a small hand.
3. Keep the eyes on the target; that is the person who is to catch the ball.
4. Practice to see how far back past the ear you will need to bring the ball.
5. Let the ball roll off the fingers with a whipping motion.
6. Follow through and have the fingers pointing toward the target at the end of the throw.

Lateral Pass

A lateral pass is one that is thrown sideways. It can be done with one or both hands. When done with one hand, it is about the same as the underarm throwing pattern. The one-handed lateral pass is not used much by young players because the ball is hard to grip.

When throwing a two-handed lateral pass, the player gets a firm grip on the ball with both hands. The player may be running with the ball and carrying it under one arm. He decides he wants to make a lateral pass to a teammate. The ball is shifted from the onearm carry to both hands. The ball is then shifted to the side of the body opposite the throw. The player brings the ball across the body and lets it go about waist high.

Catching

In football, catching is thought of as *receiving*. Those players whose main purpose is to catch the ball are called receivers. There are about three ways a ball may be caught or received in football: (1) catching while stationary, (2) catching a pass, and (3) catching a kicked ball.

Catching While Stationary

Usually a receiver will catch the ball while running. Sometimes the ball will not get to him. When that happens, he must stop and wait for the ball.

One foot is slightly ahead of the other. The feet are spread in a comfortable position. The arms and hands are extended toward the person who is passing the ball. The fingers are spread, and the hands are made into a cup.

As the ball comes toward the receiver, he transfers his weight to the foot that steps toward the ball. If the pass is high, the arms and hands move upward. The hands form a cup. When the ball is thrown low, the arms and hands move downward. The little fingers are together, and the hands again form a cup. The receiver "gives" with the ball when he contacts it. After the ball is caught, one end of it is placed under the arm above the elbow. The other hand is over the other end of the ball, and the player is now in a position to run with the ball.

Catching a Pass

Catching a forward pass is a very difficult skill. Because the receiver ordinarily catches it while running, this kind of pass requires good timing and balance.

The reader should consider again the skill of running as explained in Chapter 7. After good running skill is accomplished, the receiver is better prepared to catch a forward pass.

The body weight is forward in the running position as the ball comes in. The arms and hands move upward to make the catch. The receiver looks over his shoulder at the passer and/or the ball. The arms and fingers are extended above the shoulders. The palms of the hands face the ball. The little fingers are together, and the hands form a cup.

When the receiver gets control of the ball, he brings it down to carrying position. One end of the ball is placed above the elbow and the other hand over the end of the ball.

Catching a Kicked Ball

There are two conditions when a player may be required to catch a kicked ball. One of these is when a ball is kicked off to start the game or after a score. The other is when the ball is punted by the other team. When a ball is kicked off, it will usually come in end over end. When it is punted, it will probably come in as a spiral, as in a forward pass. (However, a punt could come in end over end if it has not been punted well.) Even though the kicked ball can approach in either of these ways, the way to catch it is about the same.

The player should try to get into a position where he thinks the ball will come down. This means trying to get lined up with the ball. The hands and arms are extended outward to form a "basket," making sure the weight is even on both feet. In the catching action, the fingers are spread apart forming a cup. The palms are upward. When contact is made with the ball the player gives with the hands and arms. The ball is pulled toward the middle of the body. As soon as there is control of the ball, it is placed under the arm and the player starts running.

Carrying the Ball

In running with the ball the ball carrier leans forward applying his best running skill. One end of the ball is placed under the arm and next to the body. There is a firm hand grip over the other end of the ball. This means that the player makes a cradle with the arm so that the ball will not fall out. When starting to run with the ball, short steps are taken. Knees are kept high to be able to change direction. Remember the skill of dodging explained in Chapter 7. It is very important for a ball carrier to be able to dodge well. When carrying the ball in an open field, longer strides are taken to get more speed.

Centering the Ball

Centering the ball is the way a play is started in football. The player who is the center passes the ball to: (1) the quarterback up close in the T formation, (2) to another player in the backfield, or (3) to the place-kick holder or punter.

In the starting position the center crouches down over the ball. The legs are spread, and one foot is a little bit behind the other. The knees are bent, and the weight is even on both feet. The right hand is placed over the front half of the ball. The left hand is on the back half of the ball. The thumbs are on top, and the fingers are on the side. The hips are about even with the shoulders.

In centering the ball to the quarterback in the T formation the ball is handed to him with one hand. In centering under conditions 2 and 3 above, just before centering the ball, the body weight moves forward toward the toes. Very little weight is on the ball. The ball is passed back with both hands between the legs. The right hand passes the ball, and the left hand guides it. After the ball is let go, the center steps forward with the back foot. He is then ready to move forward.

Punting

In the starting position the kicker stands straight with the weight on the back foot. The arms are out in front, and both hands hold the ball. The left hand is on the left side of the ball near the front. The right hand is on the right side of the ball near the back. The front part of the ball is turned a little to the left.

There is a step forward with the left foot. Next there is a step with the right foot. Then there is another step with the left foot. The arms and the ball stay in the same position during the steps. The eyes are kept on the ball. Remember that the body weight is on the foot *not* used for kicking. If the kicker is right footed, the weight is on the left foot.

When the kicking leg comes forward, the ball is let go with both hands. The ball is kicked with the top of the foot. The toes are pointed in the direction of the kick.

Place Kicking

The reader should refer back to the description of the "Stationary and Run" kick in Chapter 7. Most place kickers use what is called the "Soccer Style" kick. The kicker approaches the ball from an angle rather than head on. The kick is made with the instep with the toe pointed down and to the outer edge of the ball.

STANCE

Stance means the position a player takes before play starts. This starting position can be either a three-point stance or a four-point stance. (Sometimes players in the backfield will take a stance with their hands resting on their knees.)

In the three-point stance the feet are about shoulder width apart. One foot is slightly ahead of the other. The player takes a crouch position with the knees bent. The weight is slightly forward and resting mostly on the knuckles of one hand. The reason it is called a three-point stance is that the player is on both feet and the knuckles of one hand. The head should be up with the eyes looking straight ahead. A player can move very quickly from this position.

In the four-point stance, the weight is on both feet and the knuckles of both hands. Everything else is the same as the three-point stance, and either of these stances can be used. The stance chosen depends upon the position one is playing; that is, the line or backfield. Usually the backfield and linemen will use the three-point stance on offense. The four-point stance is used mainly by linemen on defense. The main thing, of course, is to get into the stance that is most comfortable.

BLOCKING AND TACKLING

Blocking in football means that the player gets his body in front of a player on the other team. He tries to block his path and not let his opponent get to the ball carrier. For the most part, the shoulders and hips are used in blocking. Use of the hands in blocking can sometimes be interpreted as "holding" and this is cause for a penalty.

Tackling means that one or more players bring the opposing ball carrier to the ground. A defensive player may take hold of the ball carrier on any part of the body. However, it is a penalty to take hold of the ball carrier's face mask because this can result in serious injury.

GAMES TO PRACTICE FOOTBALL SKILLS

The following games are useful to help players develop certain football skills. These games can be used as practice drills. They can also be used as substitute activities for the more highly complex game of football for those children who are not ready or do not prefer to play the game of football.

Football Keep Away

Two or more teams with any number of players can play this game. Play starts with one of the teams having the ball. This team passes the ball around to its own players. All other teams try to get the ball. When one of the teams intercepts the ball, that team gets it and tries to pass it around and keep it from the other teams. This game helps players develop the skill of handling the oval-shaped football.

Leader Ball Center Relay

Four or more players can play this game. One player is selected to be the leader. He stands with his back to the other players, who are standing in a line. The leader centers the ball to each member of the group. They return the ball to the leader. When a player misses the ball, he goes to the foot of the line. If the leader misses, he goes to the foot of the line, and the player at the head of the line replaces the leader. If desired, there can be several groups playing the game at the same time. The idea of this game is to practice the skill of centering the ball.

Football Kickball

This game requires two teams with any number on each team. The game is played on a softball diamond. All of the rules of softball are used. The ball is kicked instead of batted. The kicker stands at home plate and punts the ball. He runs to first base if the ball lands fair. All other rules of softball are used for the game. The idea of the game is to practice punting and catching punts but at the same time make a game of it.

Football Zig-Zag

There are two teams of any number of players. Each team forms a line that faces the other team. The player at one end of the line starts the game by passing to a teammate across from him. The player passes the ball back, and so on. The game goes on until the ball gets to the last player in the line. The first team to get the ball back to the leader wins. The purpose of this game is to practice the skill of forward passing, and catching as well.

Teacher Football

Any number can play this game. It is probably the best not to have more than five or six players. In this way the game goes faster, and the players get more turns. One player is selected to be the "teacher." The other players form a line facing the teacher. The teacher passes the ball to anyone in the line. If the player drops the ball, he goes to the end of the line, and the rest of the players move up. If the teacher drops the ball he goes to the end of the line, and the player at the beginning of the line becomes the teacher.

Kick and Catch

Two teams are needed for this game. There can be any number on each team. One team stands at one side of the field, and the other team stands at the other side. The game starts with the player of one team punting the ball to the other team. The player of the other team who is closest to the ball tries to catch it. If he catches it, he kicks it back. If the player misses the catch, the other team scores a point. After a certain amount of time, the team with the most points wins the game. This game gives players a chance to practice the skill of punting and also the skill of catching a kicked ball.

FLAG FOOTBALL

Flag football grew out of the game of touch football. The game of touch football grew out of the game of American football. Many people did not have a chance to engage in the game of football, the reason being that it was a very expensive game to play. So much equipment was needed that the average person did not have enough money to pay for it. Touch football provided a game where all could play without much expense.

The big difference in the game of touch football and regular football is that in touch football tackling is not allowed. This makes the game of touch football much less dangerous to play. In touch football a player is stopped by being touched rather than by being tackled. Because touching sometimes resulted in a form of pushing, which could cause injury, flag football was introduced. This game is the same as touch football except that a cloth (flag) is tucked in at the back of the waist of a player. A player is stopped when a player from the other team pulls the flag loose from the waist. This action prevents injury, and at the same time there is no question that the person was stopped. For these reasons, the game of flag football is used widely today. It is popular with girls as well as boys.

SOCCER

The game of soccer is different than most other games in that it is played mainly with the feet, while most all other games are played by using the hands to control the ball.

When the game of soccer was first started it was called *Association Football.* The rules for this game were made in the year 1863 by the *London Football Association.* Later, the word "Association" was shortened to "Assoc." which was later changed to "Soccer."

In the past few years soccer has become very popular and is played all over the world. It probably has its greatest popularity in certain South American countries. However, in more recent years it has become very popular in the United States. This popularity is particularly true of the game as played by children. In fact, my studies show that it is the fourth most popular sport among 10-year-old boys and girls.

Soccer is played on a field 130 yards by 100 yards. This is the largest the field can be. The smallest the field is supposed to be is 100 yards by 50 yards. There is a goal at each end of the field. These goals are made up of two posts, which are 8 yards apart and a crossbar on the posts, which is 8 feet above the ground. The game is played with a round heavy ball, which is about 27 to 28 inches in circumference.

To score a goal a player must get the ball through the goal and under the crossbar. This must be done with the feet or head. There are 11 players on each team and they move the ball by kicking it with their feet or hitting it with their head. There is very little use of the hands. However, the hands can be used by the goalkeeper (goalie). Also when the ball goes out-of-bounds it can be thrown in with the hands.

The game is often modified for young players. Many times a smaller playing area is used, and a much lighter ball can be used. Sometimes the rules allow for more use of the hands.

OFFENSIVE SOCCER SKILLS

There are three ways that the ball can be moved. These are (1) kicking, (2) with the head which is called "heading," and (3) with the hands to "throw in" from out-of-bounds.

Kicking

There are about six different kinds of kicks that are used in soccer: (1) kicking with the instep, (2) kicking with the inside of the foot, (3) kicking with the outside of the foot, (4) punting, (5) volley kick, and (6) foot dribbling.

Kicking with the Instep

Kicking with the instep of the foot is probably the kick that is most used in soccer. It can be used for passing the ball to a teammate and for shooting at the goal. The foot *not* used for kicking is even with the ball. The kicking leg is back, and the body leans forward a little. The ankle is downward so that the instep meets the ball.

Kicking with the Inside of the Foot

The inside edge of the foot meets the ball with the toe of the kicking foot turned out. The leg is bent slightly at the knee. When the inside of the foot meets the ball, the leg swings across in front of the body. Just as the foot meets the ball in front of the body, the knee is straightened. The foot should meet the ball just below the center. Usually the kicker takes a short run up to the ball while it is on the ground and not moving. In kicking the ball with the inside of the foot, the ball can be kicked a long way. This kind of kick can also be used to make a short pass to a teammate or to try to kick for a goal.

Kicking with the Outside of the Foot

This kick is used mainly for short distances to get the ball to a teammate. It can also be used to get the ball away from an opponent who is running toward the player. The foot that is *not* being used to kick is about 6 or 8 inches behind the ball and to the side of it. The knee of the kicking leg is bent. The kicking leg swings across in front of the other leg. The outside of the foot meets the ball as the kicking foot swings passed the other leg.

Punting

This is the kick that I called "kick from hands" in Chapter 7. The goalkeeper is the only player allowed to punt the ball. The punt is used to clear the ball over the heads of other players down the field.

Punting is a little bit like kicking with the instep. The difference is that the ball is held out in front and dropped as it is kicked. If the goalkeeper punts with the right foot, the ball is held out in front of the right leg, a little above the waist. A step is taken on the left foot and the right leg is brought back. When the ball is dropped the punter swings the right leg forward and upward. The foot hits the ball with the instep of the foot.

Volley Kick

The volley is a kick that is made while the ball is in the air. Because it is very hard to kick the ball while it is in the air sometimes the volley kick is not always allowed in soccer games with younger players. When it is used, the following is one way to do it: the player stands with the kicking foot in back of the other foot; he faces the ball as it comes in and leans forward slightly; when the ball gets to the player, the leg of the kicking foot is raised, and the weight is shifted to the other foot; the knee is bent slightly and the toes point downward; the foot meets the ball at the top of the instep, and the foot goes forward and upward.

Dribbling

Dribbling is a way to control the ball with the feet when moving along. It is a very light kick; the foot just touches the ball and moves it along.

To begin the dribble, the weight of the body is equal on both feet. The ball should be kept about one foot in front of the dribbler. The arms can be out to the side to help keep one's balance. The head should be over the ball. The ball is tapped easily with either foot. The player dribbles first with one foot and then the other. He can use the inside or outside of the foot, but it is usually easier to dribble with the inside of the foot.

Heading

Heading the soccer ball means that it is hit with the front or side of the forehead. Sometimes heading is not allowed in soccer games played by younger players. The main reason for this is that sometimes young players do not do it well, predisposing themselves to injury. If it is used, perhaps it should be done with a ball that is much lighter and softer than a regular soccer ball.

As the ball comes toward the player, the head is dropped back. The arms are raised. The weight is shifted to the back foot. The next move is to bring the body forward and upward. At this time the head meets the ball. The ball is met with the side or front of the forehead. At the end of the movement the player lands on both feet; the ankles and knees are bent; and the arms are out to the sides for balance.

The Throw In

Whenever the ball goes out-of-bounds over the sidelines it has to be put in play again. It is put in play with the *throw in* as the player stands out-of-bounds. The throw in must be done from behind the head with both hands. Part of both feet must be on the ground until the player lets the ball go.

The throw in for soccer is very much like the two-handed overhead pass in basketball, as we will see in a later chapter. The throw in is started with one foot ahead of the other. The ball is held above the head with both hands. As the ball is thrown in the player shifts the weight to the front leg. A snap of the wrists will get more force behind the ball.

DEFENSIVE SOCCER SKILLS

The way to stop the ball in soccer is called *trapping*. There are many kinds of traps, including (1) body traps, (2) foot traps, and (3) leg traps.

Body Traps

Body traps are a way to stop the ball with the body. It is done in a way so that the ball will drop to the ground at a place where the player can quickly dribble or kick it. The body trap is used when the ball is coming from a high volley, or when a player does not want a high ball to get past him.

The body is straight; the weight is on both feet; and the eyes are kept on the ball. As the ball comes in waist high or above, the body is moved backward. The weight is now on the heels, and the arms can be out to the side for balance. Just as the ball meets the body, the player should "give" with it. At the same time the player takes a short jump backward. The player tries to make a "pocket" for the ball as it hits his chest. When girls use the body trap it is a good idea for them to fold their arms over their chest. This way the ball hits their folded arms. If the body trap is done in the right way the ball will roll down the front of the player. He should then be ready to dribble or kick.

Foot Traps

Foot traps are used to stop a ball that is rolling or bouncing along the ground. The two ways to trap the ball with the feet are: (1) with the sole of the foot, and (2) with the side of the foot.

Trapping with the Sole of the Foot

The player first needs to line himself up with the ball so that it is coming straight to him. When the ball reaches the player, he raises the foot he is going to use to trap the ball. This foot is about 8 inches from the ground with the toes pointing upward. He quickly brings the sole of the foot down on the ball. The ball is trapped between the ground and the sole of the foot. It is best to use this trap when the ball is moving slowly.

Trapping with the Side of the Foot

This trap is done pretty much the same way as the trap with the sole of the foot. The main difference is in the way the ball comes to the player. It is better to use the side of the foot if the ball is bouncing from the side. Also, it might be better to use this trap when the ball is coming in fairly fast. The weight is on the foot that is *not* going to trap the ball. The player turns the foot that is to trap the ball outward so that the ball meets the inside of the foot. As soon as the ball touches the foot the player should allow the foot to "give" with the ball. With practice one should be able to make the ball stop where he wants it to stop. If the ball bounces off the foot it means that the player did not allow the foot to "give" with the ball.

Leg Traps

There are two ways of trapping the ball with the legs: (1) with one leg (or the single leg trap), and (2) with both legs (or the double leg trap).

Single Leg Trap

In the single leg trap, the player tries to get in line with the ball. The foot of the trapping leg is placed slightly in back of the other foot. Just the toes of this foot touch the ground. The knees of both legs are bent. If trapping with the right leg, the player should turn slightly to the left. When the ball meets the leg, the lower part of the leg, or shin, presses against the ball and traps it. If done correctly, the ball should be in place in front of the player where he can kick it or dribble it.

Double Leg Trap

When using the double leg trap the feet should be slightly apart with the toes pointing outward. The knees are bent slightly more than in the single leg trap. The reason for this position is to trap the ball against the ground with both shins. After the trap the body is raised up straight. The ball will be right in front where the player can dribble or kick it. It is a good idea to put the arms out to the side. This will help balance the player and keep him from falling.

TACKLING

In soccer, tackling means that the player tries to take the ball away from a player on the other team. It is called tackling the ball. When a player is good at tackling he can cause another player to make a poor kick or to overrun the ball. That is the purpose of tackling the ball in soccer. The two ways of tackling the ball are: (1) the straight tackle and (2) the hook tackle.

Straight Tackle

In the straight tackle the player tries to get in front of an opponent who is dribbling. He tries to put his foot on the ball. This movement is somewhat like trapping the ball with the sole of the foot. If one can get his foot on the ball he should try to kick it or hold it until the dribbler overruns the ball.

Hook Tackle

In the hook tackle the player also tries to get in front of the opponent who is dribbling. A quick step is taken to one side. There is a reach in with one leg and that leg is used as a "hook." The player tries to draw the ball out to the side. The other leg must be bent so as to reach in a greater distance with the hooking leg.

GAMES TO PRACTICE SOCCER SKILLS

Many of the soccer skills can be practiced by one person. In some of them it is probably better to have a partner. There are many games children can play to help them with soccer skills.

Line Soccer

In this game the players will be able to practice kicking, dribbling, and trapping. There are two teams with about eight players on a team. The playing area should be about 30 feet by 60 feet. The two teams form lines facing each other. The idea of the game is for a player to kick the ball over the other team's goal line.

To start the game, the ball is placed in the center of the playing field. Two players go to the center of the field and put their right foot on the ball. A signal is given, and each of these players tries to kick the ball across the other team's goal line. These two players can run all over the field kicking or dribbling the ball. All the other players try to keep the ball from going over the goal line. They do this by trapping or kicking the ball. Two points are scored when a player kicks the ball over the other goal line. Only the players in the center are allowed to score. The players should try to keep the ball below the waist of the other players. It is a foul if the ball is touched with the hands or arms. Kicking the ball over the head is also a foul. The penalty for a foul is a free kick, which is made from the center of the field. The game is over when everyone has had a chance to be one of the two players in the center of the field.

Corner Kickball

Corner Kickball is a good game to practice the skills of dribbling and kicking. There are two teams of about 10 players on each team. The playing area can be about 40 feet by 75 feet. The idea of the game is to kick the ball through the other team's end zone. The size of the end zone is about 15 feet from the front line to the back line.

To begin the games the ball is placed in the center of the field. On a signal, a corner player from each team runs into the center and tries to kick or dribble the ball into the other's end zone. The other players stay in the end zone and try to stop the ball with any part of their body other than their hands and arms. When a goal is scored, two other players come to the center. If a goal is not scored after a certain amount of time, two new players come to the center of the field to play the ball. It is a foul if there is tripping, pushing, or touching the ball with the hands. If there is a foul, the other team gets a free kick from 15 yards out.

Circle Trap

Any number of players can be used in this game. All of the players but one form a circle. This one player stands in the center of the circle. One of the players making the circle starts the game by rolling the ball across the circle. The players making the circle try to keep the ball moving by kicking it to one another. The player in the center of the circle tries to trap the ball. If he is able to do it, he changes places with the player who was the last one to kick the ball. If the ball goes out of the circle the one nearest it goes to the center of the circle. If the player in the center of the circle is not able to trap the ball after a period of time, another player should be chosen to go to the center.

Circle Soccer

A circle is formed with any number of players. The players kick a ball around in the circle as quickly as they can. The idea of the game is to keep the ball from going out of the circle. If the ball goes out of the circle it counts a point against the two players on either side of the ball where it went out of the circle. This means that when the ball goes out of the circle between two players each one has a point scored against him. The ball should be kept on the ground when kicking it. It should not be kicked above the waist. The game can be made more interesting by using two balls at the same time.

Hit Pin Soccer

Two teams of six to eight players each form lines about 15 feet apart. Several objects, such as ten pins, milk cartons or cans, are placed in the middle between the two teams. The players of each team kick the ball back and forth trying to knock over the objects. A point is scored when an object is knocked over. At the end of a certain amount of time, the team with the highest score is the winner.

Square Soccer

Any number of players can be used in this game. The number of players is divided into four teams. Each team stands in line side by side. All four teams make a square. The players face inward. All of the players of each team have a number; that is, if there are six players on a team one player is number one, another is number two, and so on. A leader is chosen, and he drops the ball in the center of the square. At the same time the leader calls a number. All four of the players with this number run to the center and try to get the ball through any side of the square. The players at the side of the square are goalkeepers. They can use their hands to stop the ball. As soon as a score is made by getting the ball through any side of the square, another number is called. The member of the team who got the ball through the side of the square scores a point for his team. The game can be played for a certain amount of time or until every player's number is called. Square Soccer is a good game to practice kicking, trapping, and goal tending.

Chapter 10

BASEBALL AND SOFTBALL

As mentioned elsewhere in the book, baseball has the distinction of being considered as our "national pastime." Perhaps this "pastime" is more in terms of "spectating" than participating. On the other hand, softball attracts millions of participants annually from both sexes from children to senior citizens.

BASEBALL

A form of baseball probably derived from the English games of cricket and rounders was played in the 19th century and the children's game *One Old Cat* probably existed before that. This game is played as follows: There are only two bases, first base and home base. As many as desired can be on each team. The first batter fungo bats the ball and runs to first base and back. He must make a complete trip. If he makes a complete trip without being put out, he scores a run for his team. The runner is out if a fly ball is caught or a fielder touches the runner with the ball before he reaches home. When a team makes three outs, they change places. (Fungo batting means that the batter throws the ball up himself and hits it. For a right-handed batter, the bat is held with the right hand. It can rest on the shoulder, or it can be held out to the side. The ball is held in the left hand. The weight is on the back foot. A step is taken to the side with the left foot. The ball is tossed up high enough to give time to get the left hand on the bat for the swing.) In my own childhood days One Old Cat was still a popular game, but interest in it has diminished over the years.

Baseball was played mostly in the northeastern states before the Civil War. About 1845 Alexander Cartwright set bases at about 90 feet apart. The first rule book is said to have been written by Henry Chadwick in 1858. A commission headed by A. G. Mills issued a report shortly after the turn of this century that declared that Abner Doubleday created the modern game in 1839 at Cooperstown, New York. However, it is interesting to note that this has been refuted by some authorities.[1]

When we think of children's baseball, the name *Little League* immediately comes to mind. Started in 1939, the league was originally for players 9 to 12 years of age. Little League Baseball is played on a 60 foot diamond with 46 feet from the pitching mound to the home plate. Eight-year-olds and others with less experience can play in what is called the *Minor League*. For younger children (6–8 years old) *Tee Ball* is used to help children learn the fundamentals of hitting and fielding. In Tee Ball, players hit a ball off a batting tee. Rules of the game may be varied to accomodate the need for teaching. The primary goals of Tee Ball are to instruct children in the fundamentals of baseball and to allow them to experience the value of teamwork.

In addition to Little League Baseball some of the other children's baseball leagues are: Babe Ruth, Pony Baseball, and Dixie Baseball. Some leagues make an effort to modify the game by rotating rosters every week or two so there are no team standings. In some leagues, no scores are kept in Tee Ball or "Coach-Pitch Leagues." In many leagues every player must play; in some, every player must play in the infield at least some of the time.

BASEBALL SKILLS

The most important skills in baseball are throwing, catching, batting and running. As mentioned before, running is a skill used in most games. In baseball it is used to run and field the ball and to run around the bases. The skills of catching, throwing, and batting in baseball are not easy to learn. One of the reasons for this is that players use a much smaller ball than they use in many other games. This sometimes makes the ball difficult to control.

THROWING

The skills of throwing and the patterns of throwing were explained in Chapter 7. The reader should refer back to that chapter to review these skills.

---

[1]*The New Columbia Encyclopedia*, New York, Columbia University Press, fourth edition, 1975. Eds. William H. Harris and Judith S. Levy.

Underarm Throw

In baseball sometimes the underarm throw is used as a short toss when a ball is fielded close to a base; for example, when it is fielded too close to use the overarm throwing pattern.

CATCHING

Catching in baseball is done pretty much the same way as was explained in Chapter 7. However, the ball is smaller and might be harder to control. It is a good idea to practice catching balls that are thrown than to catch a ball that is batted.

FIELDING

Catching or stopping a ball after it has been hit by a batter is called fielding. When the ball comes to the player through the air it is called a *fly ball.* When it comes along the ground it is called a *ground ball* or a *grounder.*

Fielding Fly Balls

It is important to get lined up with the ball in fielding a fly ball because the ball comes in with such force. The fielder should keep his eyes on the ball. As soon as the ball leaves the bat he should track it with his eyes. He watches the ball closely as it comes through the air and then gets ready to catch it. When the ball is high the player should try to catch it above the chin. The thumbs are together with the fingers pointing upward. When the ball drops low the player should try to catch it near the waist. The little fingers are close together. On either a high ball or low ball the player makes a little basket by spreading and cupping the fingers.

The body leans forward with the arms bent. The weight is placed evenly on both feet. If the player runs up to the ball he shifts the weight to the front foot when catching it. The bare hand follows the ball into the glove to hold the ball.

Fielding fly balls is not an easy skill, and sometimes young players may make mistakes such as the following.

1. Not lining up with the ball.
2. Running up too soon to meet the ball and thus, overrunning it.

3. Not running up soon enough to meet the ball.
4. Catching the ball with the hand in front of the eyes. When this is done the player can drop the ball because of taking the eyes off of it.
5. Trying to catch the ball with one hand under it and the other hand over it. (The hands should be side by side.)
6. Not giving with the ball. If this is not done, the ball may hit the glove and bounce out.

Fielding Ground Balls

Again it is important to get in line with the ball. For a right-handed player the left foot should be forward. The body bends at the hips, knees, and ankles, trying to keep the upper part of the body straight. The fingers point downward and the hands are placed just opposite the left foot. The player then tries to contact the ball just inside the left foot with the left hand. The ball is contacted with the right hand so that the player gets control of it. As soon as the player fields the ball he is in a position to raise the body for the throw.

PITCHING

Pitching in baseball is done with the overarm throwing pattern which was explained in Chapter 7. The following are some important things for a pitcher to remember.

1. Step toward the batter when letting the ball go.
2. Aim at target.
3. Follow through with the pitching arm.
4. At the end of the pitch, the fingers point toward the target.
5. The target is about three feet above home plate.
6. Work together with the catcher.

BATTING

Batting is a striking skill and was explained in Chapter 7. One of the first things to think about in batting is how to grip the bat. If a player is right-handed, the left hand is wrapped around the bat about two or three inches from the end. The right hand is wrapped around the bat just above the left hand. If the bat is heavy, or if it is a long bat, the player can wrap the left hand around much higher on the bat. This is called the "choke" grip. A bat should be swung several times to make sure the player is gripping it in a way that feels best.

A right-handed batter stands with the left side of the body facing the pitcher. The feet are parallel and about shoulder-width apart. The bat is held back of the head. It is about shoulder high. The arms are bent at the elbows and are held away from the body. When the ball leaves the pitcher's hand, the batter's weight should be shifted to the rear foot. If the batter decides to strike at the ball, he swings the bat forward, level with the ground. The weight is shifted to the left foot. The trade mark (printing on the bat) should be facing the batter.

Bunting

Bunting is a form of batting used to hit a ball a very short distance. Bunting can be done to surprise the fielders. It is usually done by very fast runners. They need to have a lot of speed in order to get to first base before the bunt is fielded.

In bunting, the batter should stand straight. The feet are apart so that the player can get the bat in front of the ball anywhere in the "strike zone." The left hand stays in the same place on the bat. The right hand slides about half way up the bat. There is no swing at the ball; it just hits the bat.

BASERUNNING

The skill of running as described in Chapter 7 applies much the same to baserunning. The main difference is that the runner will run only 60 feet in a straight line (the distance between bases). This distance is sometimes shortened for boys and girls at certain ages.

As soon as the ball is hit, the bat is dropped safely and the runner starts the run to first base. If he sees that he may only be able to get to first base, he should run "through" the base. If he decides that he will get more than one base, he will want to try for second base. In this case, he curves out to the right a few feet before reaching first base. In order to curve out the runner must slow down the run. The foot touches the inside of the base so that the runner will not run wide at the base.

When the baserunner is waiting on base he leans forward with the left foot on the base. If he wishes, he can "lead off" a few feet.

PLAYING THE DIFFERENT POSITIONS

In just about every team sport most members of both teams are all active at the same time. This is not the case in baseball. The batting team has one player at bat. It can have no more than three players on base. This means that at any one time the *offensive* team can have as many as four players and as few as one player active.

The fielding team or *defensive* team has nine of its players ready for action. At least they should be. Many times beginners in the game of baseball do not do well because they are not sure what they are supposed to do in their positions. The following suggests some of the things each player is supposed to do in the position he plays.

Catcher

1. He stands behind the batter in a knee-bend position.
2. He holds the glove as a target for the pitcher.
3. He fields balls that are hit close to home plate. Many times he will be the one to field a bunted ball.
4. When there is not a baserunner on first base he backs up the first baseman. This means that when the ball is hit he runs down behind first base in case the first baseman misses the ball when it is thrown to him.

Pitcher

1. He becomes a fielder when the ball is hit close to him.
2. When the first baseman is off base fielding a ball, the pitcher covers first base.
3. When there is a runner on first base, he backs up the third baseman.
4. When there is a runner on second base, he backs up the catcher.
5. He covers home plate when for some reason the catcher is drawn out of position.

First Baseman

1. He plays several feet off first base when there is no baserunner on the base and plays close to the base when there is a baserunner on first base.

2. He fields balls that are hit or thrown around the area of first base.
3. When there is not a baserunner on first base, he backs up the second baseman when throws come in from left field and center field.

Second Baseman

1. He plays between first and second base and stands several feet back of the base line and about the same distance from second base.
2. He fields balls that are hit on the left side of second base.
3. When a ball is hit to the right side of second base, he covers the base to receive the ball fielded by another player.
4. He covers second base when the ball is thrown by the catcher.
5. He goes out to receive the ball from the center fielder or the right fielder and throws it to the infield.

Shortstop

1. He plays about half way between second base and third base and stands several feet back of the base line.
2. He fields the balls that go between second base and third base.
3. When the ball is hit on the first base side of second base, he covers second base.
4. On balls thrown from the catcher he backs up the second baseman.
5. He goes out to receive the ball from the left fielder and throws it into the infield.

Third Baseman

1. He plays several feet off third base and stands about three or four feet back of the baseline.
2. He fields balls hit on the left side of the field and has to work closely with the second baseman in fielding balls.
3. On high fly balls around home plate, he sometimes comes in close to the catcher. If the catcher misses the ball he can sometimes recover it before it hits the ground.

Left Fielder

1. When balls are hit to the center field, he backs up the center fielder.
2. When he sees that it is necessary he backs up the third baseman.

Center Fielder

1. When a ball is hit to right field he backs up the right fielder.
2. When a ball is hit to left field he backs up the left fielder.
3. When a ground ball is hit to the shortstop or second baseman he backs them up.
4. He backs up the second baseman on just about all plays that come that way.

Right Fielder

1. He is the backup for the centerfielder, second baseman, and first baseman.
2. When a play is made at first base or second base, he backs it up.

TEAM PLAY

Offensive and *defensive* team play in baseball are somewhat different than in most other games. This is certainly true of offensive team play. While there is some chance for a batter and baserunner to work together, there are not a whole lot of ways where this can happen. So when we talk about offensive team play in baseball we are really talking about individual play. The following are some of the things to think about in offensive play.

1. The player should be sure to "run out" all hits. It may look like an easy out, but it is just possible that the first baseman will drop the ball. If the player has run out the hit he is more likely to be safe at first than if he did not.
2. The player should run as fast as he can and overrun first base.
3. The baserunner should be sure to know how many outs have been made when he is on base.
4. A hitter should try to be a place hitter, and try to hit the ball where the fielders are not playing.

The following are some things to remember about defensive play.

1. A player should know who to back up when a play is made.
2. A player should think ahead about what he is going to do with the ball if it is hit to him. This means that the player needs to know the number of outs and players on base.

3. A play should be made on a player who is closest to a score; that is, if a player is running for home he should try to get that player out.
4. The ball should be thrown to the base where the baserunner is going.
5. The players should talk to each other on the field so that each is sure what to do.

GAMES TO PRACTICE BASEBALL SKILLS

Many of the old neighborhood games are baseball-type games. Many children have probably played some of them at one time or another. The following games have been found useful for practicing several of the skills required in baseball.

Bases on Balls

This game is played on a softball diamond. There are two teams of any number on each team. One team is in the field while the other is at bat. A tennis ball or rubber playground ball can be used. The batter throws the ball up as in fungo batting and hits it with his hand into the field. The player in the field who gets the ball runs and places the ball on home plate. The batter runs the bases after he hits the ball. He gets a point for every base touched before the fielder places the ball on home plate. There are no outs in this game, and every player gets a chance to bat. When all players on a team have had a chance at bat, the teams change places. As many innings as desired can be played.

Hit Pin Baseball

This game is like softball except that objects such as ten pins or empty milk cartons are used rather than bases. The pitcher throws the ball in easily so that the batter can hit it. When the batter hits the ball he starts around the bases. The fielder who gets the ball throws it to first base. The first baseman knocks the object over with the ball and throws the ball to second base. The game goes on until the ball has gone around all the bases and the objects have been knocked down. The batter stops when the object (base) he is headed for is knocked down. There are no outs, and every member of the team gets to bat in each inning.

Base Run

There are four players on a team in this game. These players are a catcher, first baseman, second baseman, and third baseman. The catcher stands at home base, and the basemen are on their bases. There is a runner who tries to get around the bases once while the ball goes around twice. The runner starts when the catcher throws the ball to first. The first baseman throws the ball to second, and so on. The baserunner tries to beat the ball. If the runner gets around once before the ball gets around twice he scores one point for his team. After the four runners have had a chance to run, they become the basemen.

Beatball Baseball

This game can have seven or more players on each team. If the batter hits the pitch he runs to first, second, third, and home without stopping. The fielders get the ball to the first baseman, who must touch the base with the ball in his hands. The first baseman throws the ball to the second baseman on base. The second baseman throws to the third baseman on base. The third baseman throws to the catcher. If the ball gets home before the runner, then he is out. The ball must beat the runner home and not just the bases ahead of the runner. If the runner beats the ball home he scores a run for his team. All of the other rules of baseball apply.

Flies and Grounders

Any number of players can play this game. There is one batter, and the other players go into the field. The batter fungo bats the ball into the field. The player closest to the ball can go for it, and he calls out, "Mine!" If he catches it on the fly, it counts five points. If he catches it on first bounce from a fly, it counts three points. If he catches a grounder, it counts one point. When a player gets 15 points, he becomes the batter.

SOFTBALL

Softball was started in the early 1900s by American professional baseball players. They played softball to keep in practice during the offseason. At that time the game was called *Indoor Baseball.* During the late 1920s the game became very popular in Canada. Players from that country began to play the game outdoors on playgrounds and it became known as *Playground Ball.* Sometime later the game was changed to *Softball,* and that is the name it goes by today.

It was not long before there was a great deal of interest in the game in the United States. This interest actually started about 1930. The game is now played by millions of men and women and boys and girls all over the country. Although both boys and girls enjoy playing softball, it is a favorite of girls by a ratio of almost 5 to 1. Little League started a softball program for ages 9 to 12 in 1974.

The size of the softball can be from 12 inches to 32 inches in circumference. For young players the distance of the baseline is arbitrary. Ordinarily, the larger the ball the shorter the baselines are likely to be.

The skills for softball are essentially the same as they are for baseball. One main exception is pitching. Pitching is done with the underarm throwing pattern, which was explained in Chapter 7. At the start of the pitch the feet should be parallel. The ball is held with both hands, and the pitcher faces the batter. For a right-handed pitcher, the right arm is swung back. The body turns slightly. The right arm is brought forward, and the ball is let go off the ends of the fingers. The ball should be at about the level of the hip when it is pitched. The right foot is brought up so that the pitcher is in good position to field the ball if it is hit by the batter.

Chapter 11

BASKETBALL AND VOLLEYBALL

A distinguishing characteristic about basketball and volleyball is that both games had their origin in the United States. In fact, they were invented within four years of each other in the late 19th century.

BASKETBALL

Sometimes people wonder how certain games got their start and how they got their name. Many games that we play began in other countries. Basketball is one of the few games that got its start in the United States.

The game was invented by Doctor James Naismith in Springfield, Massachusetts in 1891. When he was a student, the teacher of one of his classes had suggested an assignment that involved the invention of a game that could be played indoors with a small number of players. Doctor Naismith invented the game of basketball for the class assignment, and also that there would be a game that could be used to fill in time between the end of football season in the fall and the start of baseball in the spring.

In the beginning, the game of basketball was much different than it is today. There were nine players on each team. They were allowed to throw, bat, or pass the ball. The first game was played with peach baskets, and this is how it got the name of basketball. After a time, the rules changed so that there were five on a men's team and six on a women's team. In modern times there are also five on women's teams. In the early days the number of players sometimes depended on how much space there was for playing.

In the beginning the game was played by only grown men and women. Today it is played by children as well as adults, although the rules may be simpler for young players than they are for adults.

Interest in the game of basketball has spread so much that it is now played in many countries around the world. In fact, it has become a very

166

important part of the Olympic Games. People of all ages seem to enjoy trying to put a ball through a basket.

Basketball as played today can take place on a court as small as 42 feet by 72 feet. The largest size is 50 feet by 90 feet. The basketball goals at either end of the court are 10 feet high with each team having its own goal. It is interesting to note that this is one dimension of the game that has never changed; that is, when the game began the goal was 10 feet and this height still remains the same today. Sometimes for young players the goals may be eight or nine feet. This shorter height can make it easier for them to get the ball into the basket. The regular size of the ball is 29½ inches around. Smaller balls of 29 inches around are used for players under high school age. Even much smaller balls can be used because they are easier for younger players to handle. In this general regard, Benham[1] reviewed the literature regarding the effect that scaling down equipment has on a child's basketball performance. It was concluded that: (1) a decrease in the basketball size and weight appears to benefit young children with less absolute body size and strength by requiring less force to be applied when shooting or passing and improved ball control skills, and (2) a decrease in the goal height appears to benefit children's shooting accuracy.

The popularity of basketball among children apparently is surpassed by no other sport. For example, recently when 7,500 children were asked in a *Sports Illustrated For Kids* poll to name their favorite athlete and the athlete they would like to be for a day, their three top choices were professional basketball players Michael Jordan, Magic Johnson, and Scottie Pippen. Larry Bird and Charles Barkely were also in the top ten. This is also borne out in my own studies which consistently show that basketball is by far the most popular sport among 9 to 12 year olds.

BASKETBALL SKILLS

The game of basketball requires many different kinds of skills. These skills include, passing, catching, shooting, dribbling, pivoting, and guarding.

---

[1]Benham, Tami, Modifications of Basketball Equipment and Children's Performance, Paper presented at the *National Convention of the American Alliance for Health, Physical Education and Dance,* Cincinnati, Ohio, April 10-13, 1986.

PASSING

Passing simply means that the ball is transferred from one player to another. There are many different kinds of passes and each one has its own purpose. The kind of pass used will depend on two things. The first thing is the distance the ball has to travel. Second, the position in which the ball is caught may cause the player to choose the kind of pass to make. The following are some of the more widely used passes.

Chest Pass

This pass is probably the one most often used in basketball. It is good to use when the ball is to be passed a short distance. The ball is held chest high. The fingers grip the ball and are spread lightly over the center of the ball. The thumbs are close together. The elbows are bent and close to the body. In the passing action the arms go forward from the shoulders and the elbows straighten. The ball is let go with a snap of the wrists. The ball can be passed a greater distance if the knees are bent and a short step is taken with one foot.

Bounce Pass

This pass can be done with one or both hands. It is probably better to use both hands as this makes it easier to control the ball. In this pass, a bounce is used so that the ball can bounce into the other player's hands. When two hands are used, it is done about the same way as the chest pass. The difference is that the ball is passed low to hit the floor rather than chest high. This is not an easy pass to make, and it takes lots of practice. The passer must judge the place on the floor to bounce the ball. It is a good idea to make the ball hit the floor about three-fourths of the distance from the passer to the catcher. This kind of pass will cause the ball to be caught at about the waist. Some beginners make the mistake of bouncing the ball straight downward rather than pushing it forward. The good feature about the bounce pass is that it sometimes allows the passer to get the ball to the catcher before it can be blocked.

One-Handed Underarm Pass

This pass is done with the underarm throwing pattern explained in Chapter 7. Because the ball is too big to be gripped, the other hand is put on top of the ball. This will keep the ball from falling out of the throwing hand. The other hand is taken away when the ball is brought forward. This pass is good to use for short distances to get the ball quickly to another player.

Shoulder Pass

This pass is sometimes called the *baseball pass* or the *one-hand overarm pass.* It is done with the overarm throwing pattern explained in Chapter 7. This pass is not used too often by young players because it is hard to control. It is useful when passing a distance. If a teammate breaks away and gets down the floor it can be a good pass to get the ball there more quickly. It should be remembered that as a general rule short passes are better than long ones. It should also be remembered that the longer the pass the better chance it has to be caught by a member of the other team.

The shoulder pass is begun with one foot just ahead of the other. The hand that is not used to throw the ball is used to steady it. This helps the passer to keep from losing control of the ball. The ball is brought forward above the shoulder and past the ear. When the ball is let go there should be a snap of the wrist the same as in the chest pass.

Two-Handed Overhead Pass

The reader may recall that this is the pass used for the "throw in" in soccer. The ball is held over the head with both hands. It is about one foot in front of the head. The fingers are spread above the center of the ball, and the elbows are slightly bent. The passer steps forward with one foot and passes the ball forward at the same time. At the end of the pass the arms and fingers will be pointing upward. This is a good pass to use when the distance is longer than is needed for the chest pass.

CATCHING

The reader might wish to review the general discussion about catching in Chapter 7. Some of those procedures will be repeated because of the way they apply to basketball. An important factor in catching in the game of basketball is that the catcher should move to meet the ball. This movement is sometimes called *cutting* and will shorten the distance the ball has to travel. Also, it will help to shut off a player of the other team who tries to block the ball. When the ball is caught it should be brought in as close to the body as possible. This will help to keep the person who is guarding the passer from getting the ball.

It has already been mentioned how the hands should be held when a ball is caught at the waist, above the waist, or below the waist. Usually a basketball is caught in the last two positions, above or below the waist. When catching a basketball above the waist the hands are forward toward the ball with fingers pointing up. The knees are slightly bent; the feet are apart; and the body leans slightly forward. When the ball is caught the fingers are spread, and the hands and arms give with the ball. This helps to slow down the force of the ball and makes it easier to control.

In catching the basketball below the waist, the fingers point downward and are well spread and the hands and arms give with the ball when it is caught. The player should try not to shift the hands on the ball because he might want to pass it quickly with the same motion.

SHOOTING

Because putting the ball through the hoop is the method of scoring, shooting is obviously one of the most important skills.

The basic patterns of basket shooting are those of throwing which were discussed in Chapter 7. Three things need to be remembered. First, allowance must be made for the angle when the ball is released. The second thing is how much force is needed to send the ball to the basket. The third important thing to remember is that the eyes should be kept on the rim of the goal.

There are about five different kinds of shots in the game of basketball that will be discussed here.

1. Two-handed underhand shot.
2. Two-handed chest shot.
3. One-handed push shot.
4. Lay-up shot.
5. Jump shot.

Two-Handed Underhand Shot

This is probably the easiest way for young players to shoot. It could be useful as a free throw shot. If used as a shot while the ball is in play, it is easy to block. The ball is held about waist high. The fingers of both hands are under the ball with the thumbs pointing upward. The knees are bent and the ball is brought downward between the legs. The ball is then brought upward, and the knees become straight. The ball is released when the arms are straight toward the basket.

Even though it is a good way to shoot free throws, most players of high school age and older use other kinds of shots for free throws. One big exception was Rick Barry, the former basketball star of the Houston Rockets. He used the two-handed underhand shot for free throws, and the fact that he was one of the best "foul shooters" in all of basketball is reason enough for believing that it is a good way to shoot free throws.

Two-Handed Chest Shot

This shot is a good one for beginners because the ball is easy to control. The two-handed chest shot is like the chest pass, but the angle where the ball is released is different. The ball is held in both hands about chest high. The ball is tipped back on the fingers, which are spread and above the center of the ball. The ball is then pushed toward the goal. The shooter tries to get a proper arch on the flight of the ball. Either foot can be ahead of the other, or the feet can be together. The knees should be bent. When the ball is released the legs are straightened. At the end of the shot, the arms are stretched, and the fingers point upward toward the basket.

One-Handed Push Shot

The ball is balanced by the fingers of the shooting hand. The other hand supports the ball from underneath. One foot is slightly ahead of the other. The knees are bent slightly and the feet are spread at a distance where the shooter feels comfortable. Most of the weight is on the front foot. The hand underneath the ball is taken away as the ball is pushed toward the basket. When the ball is released, the fingers of the shooting hand point toward the basket. The arm is stretched to full length upward. This shot may not be easy because it is harder to control the ball with one hand than it is with two. However, if the shooter can control the ball, this shot is hard to guard against, the reason being that the shot starts high and the shooter can release the ball quickly.

Lay-Up Shot

This shot is a little bit like the one-handed push shot. The ball is aimed at the backboard when the shooter is close in under the basket. The reason for this aim is that the ball is banked against the backboard into the basket; that is, the shooter "lays" the ball on the backboard. The right-handed shooter takes off close to the basket from the left foot and jumps as high as possible toward the goal. For the left-handed shooter the takeoff is with the right foot. The player usually comes to the basket from the side with a bounce of the ball, or he may catch a pass from a teammate as he runs in. It is probably a good idea to practice the shot first without the jump. This will give the shooter an idea of where the ball should hit the backboard so that it will drop into the basket.

Jump Shot

The jump shot uses the same movement as the one-handed push shot. The shot is made after jumping into the air from the floor with both feet. The jump shot is difficult to guard against because the ball is higher when the shooter releases it. At the same time it is a difficult shot to make and takes a great deal of practice.

DRIBBLING

Dribbling means that a player controls the ball by bouncing it several times. The fingers are well spread so that it will be easier to control the ball. The knees are bent to keep the body low. The body leans forward; the ball is held just a little higher than the knees. The beginning dribbler will probably need to keep the eyes on the ball. After the skill is learned, the player should practice keeping the head up. The first bounce is started by laying the ball well out in front and pushing with the dribbling hand. The ball is pushed forward the floor and not slapped downward.

PIVOTING

The basic skill of pivoting was described in Chapter 7. In basketball, pivoting is used to change direction when a player is standing in place. It takes place when a player who is holding the ball steps once, or more, in any direction with the same foot. The other foot is the pivot foot and stays in contact with the floor. The weight of the body is equally placed on both feet. The ball is held firmly with the finger tips of both hands. The elbows point outward to help protect the ball from a player on the other team. The player can turn in any direction on the pivot foot. He should not drag the pivot foot because this movement is the same as walking with the ball (traveling).

GUARDING

Up to this point the discussion has been about skills with the ball. The skill of guarding is used to try to keep an opponent from shooting, passing, or dribbling. An important rule in guarding is that the player should try to keep between the basket and the player he is guarding. In guarding, the feet are spread, and the knees are bent. The arms are outstretched to the sides. One arm can be up and the other arm down. In this position the player is ready to move in any direction. That movement is usually done with the skill of sliding, which was described in Chapter 7. When the person a player is guarding gets the ball the player should try to get about two or three feet away from him. In guarding position the player is ready not only to block a pass or shot, but also to stop a dribble.

REBOUNDING

When a shot does not go into the basket it will probably rebound back to the playing area; that is, if it does not go out of bounds. Rebounding is a skill used to try to get the ball after it has bounced off the backboard or the basket. This is one of the most difficult skills to learn. The reason for this is that the player must time the jump and rebound of the ball. A player who is able to time these two movements well will be in the right spot to get the ball. The player jumps from the floor and stretches the arms toward the basket. If the ball is caught it should be brought in close to the body. When the player has the ball and the feet are on the floor, he should bend forward to protect the ball. If a person is successful in rebounding at his own basket his team will control the ball. Getting a rebound at the other team's basket means that a player will have taken the ball so that the other team cannot shoot again right away. Although it helps to be tall in rebounding, being able to jump high and time the jump are also very important.

TEAM PLAY

The most important thing in basketball is team play. This means both offensive and defensive team play. The following are some important things to remember about offensive team play.

1. Players should try to be aware at all times where their teammates are on the floor.
2. Players should be thinking about getting into an empty space to get away from their guard.
3. When a player passes the ball he should keep moving and not stand around.
4. Players will usually have more success with short passes than with long ones.
5. When shooting, the player should make sure that he has a good chance of making the basket; otherwise, he should pass to another player.
6. When a player has the ball there are only three things he can do. He can pass, shoot, or dribble. He must decide quickly what is the best thing to do. If he does not have a good shot it is a good idea to pass the ball. Dribbling should probably be used only when, for some reason, the player is not able to pass the ball.

The following are some important things to remember about defensive play.

1. Most guarding is done in the other team's offensive area of the floor. Usually there is little need to guard all over the floor. There are certain times like near the end of the game to use a pressing defense (guarding all over the floor).
2. A player should always know who he is supposed to guard.
3. When guarding, a player should never cross his feet. The skill of sliding should be used instead.

4. It may be a good idea to have one person stay back to guard near the other team's basket.
5. In guarding, the player should always try to keep between the basket and the player he is guarding.

GAMES TO PRACTICE BASKETBALL SKILLS

Most of the skills that have been discussed can be practiced by one person alone. However, with some of them it is better to have a partner. If there are several people, they can play games to practice the skills.

The games that are explained here are just a few examples of many possibilities. Many times players can make up games of their own that are good for practicing certain basketball skills. The following games use one or more of the skills of passing, catching, dribbling, shooting, and guarding. They do not need to be played on a regular basketball court.

Bear in the Circle

Two circles are formed with each circle as a team with four or more players. A member of the other team, the bear, stands in the center of each circle. The players in the circle pass the ball around, and the bear tries to touch it. If the bear touches the ball, a point is scored for that team. To begin with, players decide how long they will play the game. At the end of that time the team with the highest score is the winner. Everyone on both teams should have a turn at being the bear.

Keep Away

There can be as many teams as desired in this game with four or more players on a team. It is better to have more teams so that there are not many players on a team. This way more players will get a chance to handle the ball. Play starts with one of the teams having the ball. This team passes the ball around to its own players. Players of all the other teams try to get the ball. If a member of one of the teams gets the ball, that team starts play again with the ball. All of the rules of basketball are used, and the idea of the game is to see which team can keep the ball for the longest amount of time.

Tag Ball

This game is like *Keep Away* except that one member on each of the teams is picked to be *It*. The purpose of the game is to tag the person on a team who is *It* with the ball. When this happens the tagging team scores a point. All of the rules of basketball are used. The ball can be advanced to *It* by passing or dribbling. All players who are *It* should stand out in some way, perhaps with an armband, so that the others can tell easily which players are *It*.

Half-Court Basketball

All the rules of basketball are used. The only difference from the regular game is that only one-half of the court is used. Both teams use the same goal. When a goal is made or the other team gets the ball, the other team must start again with the ball. Play usually begins again somewhere around the free throw line or in the center of the court. This is a good game if one has a basketball goal in the yard or in the driveway.

VOLLEYBALL

Like basketball, the game of volleyball got its start in the United States. It was invented in 1895, four years after the game of basketball. The game was invented by William Morgan while he was teaching at the YMCA in Holyoke, Massachusetts.

The reader may recall that basketball was started as an indoor game that could be used to fill in between the end of football season in the fall and baseball season in the spring. It is believed that Mr. Morgan started the game of volleyball for those who were not interested in playing basketball.

Today, volleyball is one of the world's leading sports. One of the reasons for its popularity is that it is a game that can be played by people of all ages. Young and old alike seem to get a great deal of enjoyment out of hitting the ball back and forth across the net. While it started out as an indoor game, it is now played on playgrounds, in parks, on the beach, as well as many other places. Volleyball has become so popular that millions of people of all ages all over the world play the game. It has become one of the very important team sports in the Olympic Games.

The game got its name because the ball is volleyed back and forth across a net with the hands. This action is called volleying. The idea of the game is to volley the ball back and forth with each team trying to score points. Points are scored by placing the ball in such a way that the other team cannot return it before it hits the surface area.

The game is played on a court 60 feet in length by 30 feet in width. A net is placed over the middle of the court at a height of eight feet (sometimes the net is lowered to seven feet for women). The net can be placed at any height for young players, depending on their age and skill. For beginners, a lightweight plastic ball or beachball can be used.

There are six players on a team. Three of these are in the front line, and three are in the back line. Players change their positions on the court at certain times during the game. This gives all players a chance to play in different positions in the front line and the back line. The ball can be hit three times by players on one team. The third person to hit it must get it over the net. One player cannot hit the ball two times in succession. It does not have to be hit three times, but it is usually best to do so. The reason for this is that it makes for better team play.

In 1971 the game of mini-volleyball was developed. This game is about the same as regular volleyball except that it is played on a smaller court. The net is usually five to six feet in height. There are three or four players on a side. In many places, younger players take part in mini-volleyball before they get into the regular game of volleyball. In many countries the beginning age for starting to play volleyball is nine years. It has been found that mini-volleyball is best for boys and girls of this age.

VOLLEYING

Sometimes volleying is called passing because it is the way the ball is passed from one player to another and over the net. Although the ball should be volleyed and not caught, for beginners it is a good idea to catch the ball and throw it back and forth. The main thing is that the ball not be held too long after it is caught. The player should let it go more quickly each time. Before long players will be able to volley the ball, and they will be likely to find that it will be easier to volley the ball if they start out by throwing it. Sometimes for beginners the rules allow the ball to bounce one time before it is volleyed. This is easier for some boys and girls than it is to hit the ball on the fly.

There are three kinds of volleys discussed here: (1) overhead volley, (2) underhand volley, and (3) forearm volley.

Overhead Volley

Some people consider the overhead volley the most important volley-ball skill for young players to learn. The reason for its importance is that it is the volleying skill that is probably used the most. It is used when the ball comes in chest high or higher. It is a difficult skill and takes lots of practice.

The hands are held at about the level of the eyes. The fingers are spread with the thumbs almost touching each other. A little window is formed between the thumbs. The elbows are bent and out about the height of the shoulders. The player takes a crouch position so that the ball will come in toward the eyes. The knees are bent enough to be in a comfortable position; one foot should be slightly ahead of the other. When the ball is contacted with the fingers and thumbs, the weight should be even on the balls of the feet. The player strikes the ball upward in the direction he is aiming. This will most likely be to a teammate if the player is the first or second person to volley the ball. The player should try to volley the ball as high as 12 to 15 feet from the floor. Some beginners make the following mistakes in the overhead volley.

1. The ball is slapped rather than pushed.
2. The ball is hit more forward than upward.
3. The body is straight when the ball is hit rather than in a crouch.
4. Using one hand instead of both.
5. The player fails to get lined up with the ball.

Underhand Volley

The underhand volley is no longer used in the game of volleyball. However, it is good to practice before trying the forearm volley. The knees are bent with the feet apart. The hands are below the waist with the palms facing upward. The fingers point downward with the little fingers together. The eyes are watching the ball. When the ball is contacted, the body weight is even on the balls of the feet. With the hands together the player strikes the ball upward. The arms, body and legs are extended.

The movement is completed by following through with the arms and body in the direction of the ball to finish the volley.

Forearm Volley

The forearm volley is also called the *bump* or the *dig*. This volley is used mainly for four kinds of plays: (1) when the ball is low and below the waist, (2) to receive most serves, (3) to recover the ball off the net, and (4) when the player's back is toward the net.

One of the first things to consider in the forearm volley is the position of the hands. One hand is placed in the palm of the other hand. The thumbs are on top, and one thumb is placed over the other. The forearms are very close together. The body is in line with the ball, and the knees are bent. One foot can be slightly ahead of the other. The arms are lowered to prepare to receive the ball. The ball should bounce off the inside of the forearms and wrists. At the time the ball contacts the forearms it should be allowed to bounce rather than be met hard with the forearms. When contact is made with the ball, the body moves a little in the direction of the ball. It is a good idea to try to keep the ball high in the air.

SERVING

Serving is the way the ball is put into play. It means that the ball is hit with the hand by the player who is the server. The server is allowed to serve the ball from either the underhand position or the overhand position. The hand may be open or closed. Young players should begin with the underhand serve. After they have been able to serve well with the underhand serve they might want to try the overhand serve. Some younger players can do well with the overhand serve. Others may have a difficult time with it and prefer to stay with the underhand serve.

Underhand Serve

The player stands facing the net. The left foot is a little ahead of the right foot. If the player is left-handed he should have the right foot ahead. The weight is on the rear foot. The body bends slightly forward. The ball is held in the left hand. It is in front and a little to the right of the body and the right hand should be lined up with the ball.

The serving motion is the same as the underarm throwing pattern explained in Chapter 7. The right arm swings forward and contacts the ball just below the center of it. The ball can be hit with the open hand or with the fist. If hit with the open hand, it should be with the heel of the fist. This means that the hand forms a fist with the thumb and index finger upward. To complete the serve the player follows through with the arm in the path of the ball. He can also step forward with the right foot after the serve.

Overhand Serve

In the overhand serve the right-handed server stands with the left foot in front. The left side is turned slightly toward the net. The ball is held in the palm of the left hand. The ball is about chest high. The weight is equal on both feet. The eyes watch the ball. The ball is tossed up two or three feet into the air above the right shoulder. When the toss is made, the weight shifts to the back foot. When the ball begins to drop, the weight is shifted to the forward foot. The arm is snapped forward, and the ball is contacted about a foot above the shoulder. The contact is made near the center of the ball with the tips of the fingers or fist. The overhead serving action is about the same as the overarm throwing pattern used in baseball or softball.

THE SET

The set means that the ball is set up for a teammate to hit it over the net. The set is usually the second hit. The ball is set up high for a teammate to spike it down over the net. In setting up the ball, the overhead volley is used. The ball should be volleyed up at a height of 12 to 15 feet. It is set up about one foot away from the net.

THE SPIKE

A spike means that the ball is hit downward as it goes into the other team's side of the court. It is a very important scoring skill, but it is very hard to learn. The player who is going to spike the ball stands close to the net. He faces the direction from where the ball is coming. When the ball starts to come down, the spiker jumps high off the floor. He swings his right arm downward while it is still above the net. He should try to hit the ball on the top to get more force behind it. The spiker lands facing the net. He should be sure not to let his hand go over the net. Since this skill is very difficult to learn, it is a good idea to practice spiking the ball with the net down fairly low.

THE BLOCK

The block is used against a spike. The player who is going to try to block the spike faces the net. He tries to jump at the same time the spiker does. He swings both arms upward with the hands close together. He should try to get about six inches above the net. If the blocker is unsuccessful, the ball will bounce off his hands and back into the other team's side of the court. Probably the hardest part about this skill is learning to jump just at the right time.

NET RECOVERY

Sometimes a teammate will hit the ball into the net on his side of the court. A player tries to recover the ball so that it will not hit the floor. If there have been one or two hits, a player can hit the ball as it bounces off the net. He faces the net and watches it closely when the ball is going to hit. He uses the forearm volley to try to get the ball up high.

TEAM PLAY

Volleyball is a game in which there is a very quick shift back and forth from offense to defense. This is because the ball goes back and forth across the net very quickly.

A team scores only on its own serve. This means that when a team serves and, after one or more volleys back and forth over the net, the ball lands on the other team's side, the serving team scores a point. If the ball lands on the serving team's side of the court there would be no score for the other team because it was not the serving team.

The following are several important things to remember about offensive play.

1. The server should try to place the ball in an open space. It is also a good idea to try to serve it near the end of the court and close to the side line.

2. The ball must go over the net on the third hit. There is usually better team play when the three hits are taken.

3. A three-hit play might go as follows: the ball is received by a back-line player; his hit is the first one, and it goes to a front-line player; this player makes the second hit and sets it up for a teammate to spike it; and the third hit is the spike over the net. This three-hit play takes a lot of practice and teamwork.

4. It is not a good idea for the front-line players to play with their backs to the net. They should either face the net or turn the body only about halfway around.

5. Try to volley the ball high.

The following are some of the important things to remember about defensive play.

1. Always try to keep the eyes on the ball.

2. Usually try to keep one foot ahead of the other with the weight equal on both feet.

3. Most of the time a serve will be received by a back-line player. This player should volley the ball to a front-line player.

4. Sometimes if the serve is short, it can be received by a front-line player. If a player on the front line has to jump too high for the ball, he should let it go to a back-line player.

5. Just like in the game of baseball and softball, certain players back up other players in volleyball. The player at the right in the back line backs up the player at the right in the front line. The player in the center of the back line backs up the player in the center in the front line. The player at the left in the back line backs up the player at the left in the front line.

6. The player should call out "Mine" or "My ball" if he is going to take the ball. Calling out will help keep two teammates from running into each other to get the ball.

GAMES TO PRACTICE VOLLEYBALL SKILLS

It was mentioned before that there are six players on a regular volleyball team. There are three players in the front line and three players in the back line. The three players in the front line are the right forward, center forward, and the left forward. The three players in the back line are the right back, center back, and left back. In the following games any number can play. In these games it is not necessary to always follow the regular rules of volleyball. The idea for these games is to learn certain skills that can help make one a better volleyball player.

Net Ball

Net ball is played about the same as volleyball except that the ball is *thrown* back and forth across the net. The purpose is to get the players used to getting the ball over the net. If a player drops the ball, it counts a point for the other team. There can be as few as one player on a side; however, it is better to have three or more players on each side.

Keep It Up

Two or more teams of players with three or four players on a team can play this game. Each team forms a circle. On a signal, each team starts to volley the ball. The players on a team volley it to each other. They can use any kind of volley to do this. When one of the teams allows the ball to hit the ground, it counts a point against that team.

Serve Up

Two people can play this game, or more can play if desired. The ball is served to a partner and he serves it back. They start out a short distance apart and then keep making the distance longer.

Volley Up

This game is the same as Serve Up except that the ball is volleyed back and forth rather than being served back and forth. A player tries to see how many good volleys he can get without letting the ball hit the ground.

Wall Volleyball

From two to four players can play this game. The idea of the game is to keep the ball bouncing against a wall. One player starts by serving against the wall. It is returned by the next player. Play goes on with the players taking turns hitting the ball. After the serve, the ball is volleyed against the wall. If a player allows the ball to hit the ground, the player who last hit the ball against the wall scores a point.

Volleyball Keep Away

Two teams with any number of players on a team can play this game. It is a good idea to have at least three players on a team. The team members try to volley the ball to each other. The other team tries to get the ball. If it does, the players try to volley it to each other. The team that volleys the ball the greatest number of times wins the game. This is a good game to play with a beachball.

Chapter 12

INDIVIDUAL SPORTS

M ost individual sports provide for a situation in which one competes against himself or herself and natural forces. This form of challenge may be one of the reasons why individual sports are popular among children—particularly those in the 10–12 year age range. Moreover, it is interesting to note that individual sports are more popular with girls than boys by a ratio of almost two to one.

In reality, one could say that the so-called individual sports are at once also team sports because a winner is often declared on a team basis by total team points. For example, it is common practice to refer to track teams, bowling teams, and so on. The one aspect that sets individual sports apart from team sports is the absence of teamwork in the individual sports.

The individual sports that I have selected for discussion are those that emerged as most popular among children in my studies—swimming, track and field, and gymnastics—and golf, which has recently had a widespread gain in popularity with children. This should not be interpreted to mean that these are the only individual sports of interest to children, because many children engage in and enjoy a host of other individual sports.

SWIMMING

It is believed that swimming is one of man's oldest activities, probably dating back to prehistoric times. It is mentioned in many of the classics in connection with heroic acts of religious rites. It is interesting to note that the first book on methods of swimming was *Dialogue Concerning the Art of Swimming* by Nicholas Wynman published in 1538.[1]

---

[1] *The New Columbia Encyclopedia*, New York, Columbia University Press, Edited by William H. Harris and Judith S. Levy, 1975.

Many people are of the opinion that one of the most unique features about swimming is that it uses more muscles with precise coordination than almost any other sport.

The reader may recall that in my discussion of the historical background of children's sports in Chapter 1, I mentioned that John Locke, the famous 17th century British philosopher, proclaimed that children should learn to swim early in life. Without question this is still a theory that exists in modern times. The question to pose is: "How early in life?"

Mary Carter,[2] Assistant Acquatics Director at the Silver Spring, Maryland YMCA, who for many years has been teaching children to swim, suggests that the optimum age to learn to swim is between four and five. She contends that the greatest fear of water is often seen in those children who have not learned to swim until they are seven or eight.

The emerging interest of swimming programs for young children has been accompanied by an increasing volume of literature on the subject. The following comments by Virginia C. Reister and Andrew J. Cole[3] is a case in point. They maintain that early childhood programs are being offered by the American Red Cross and the YMCA with its Y Skippers Program for children five years old and younger. These programs are aimed at safety and education of parents. Most of the programs are not aimed at teaching young children to swim per se; instead, they are oriented to familiarization, the development of component skills, enjoyment, and of course, concern for safety. Another aspect of early childhood programs is the advantage of physical activity at an early age, the development of motor skills, and the socialization that results from group programs.

Many swimming enthusiasts and parents as well tend to believe that these experiences are important to child development. In this regard, Stephen Langendorfer[4] an expert on the subject suggests that long-term developmental studies of infants and young children who have experienced aquatic programs are needed to answer this most crucial question: Does early aquatic and/or movement experience really enhance the total development of the child?

---

[2]Squires, Sally, How to Conquer Kids' Fear of Submerging, Washington, DC, Washington Post Health, August 18, 1992.

[3]Reister, Virginia C. and Cole, Andrew J., Start Active, Stay Alive in the Water, *Journal of Physical Education, Recreation and Dance,* January 1993.

[4]Langendorfer, Stephen, Aquatics for the Young Child, Facts and Myths, *Journal of Physical Education, Recreation, and Dance,* August 1986.

As far as competitive swimming for children is concerned, some of our recent Olympians started swimming at about age six and by the age of eight were competing in meets. In this connection one writer on the subject, Irene Christie,[5] has observed that the physical advantages of competitive training programs in swimming for children are positive if physiological factors of growth and development are observed.

Most of what we have on the subject is more or less subjective opinion. And this needs to be fortified insofar as possible by objective research.

TRACK AND FIELD

Track and field events may be among the world's oldest sports activities. In ancient Greece track and field dominated the Olympic Games. Such organized contests were also popular in Rome but interest lapsed in the early Middle Ages. In England, these activities were revived in the 12th century with continuing interest. The first college track and field meet occurred in England in 1864, with Oxford and Cambridge Universities as the competitors. It was around this time that track and field became popular in the United States.[6]

Interest in track and field among children got its start with the advent of the public school "Field Day" in some of our large metropolitan areas during the latter part of the 19th century. This activity ordinarily occurred during the spring near the end of the school year. Popular events included short running races, jumping events, and throwing a baseball for distance. Many elementary schools throughout the country still carry on this tradition because of the great interest and enjoyment it provides for children.

At the present time various organizations provide track and field sports for children. Prominent among these is the Junior Olympics Program. This program takes place during the summer and is designed to provide instructions and competition in track and field for children 6–18 years of age. The program has six divisions as follows: Pee Wees (ages 6–7), Bantams (ages 8–9), Midgets (ages 10–11), Youths (ages 12–13), Intermediates (ages 14–15), and Young Men and Women (ages 16–18). Activities are appropriately modified for the various ages groups.

---

[5]Christie, Irene, Children in Competitive Swimming, Effects of Hard Training, *Physical Educator*, October 1984.

[6]*The New Columbia Encyclopedia*, New York, Columbia University Press, Edited by William H. Harris and Judith S. Levy, 1975.

As far as modification is concerned, there is usually an attempt to do so for track and field events in the same manner as activities are "scaled down" for children from adult standards in other sports. In this regard, Werner and Almond[7] have recommended a three-phase framework to help coaches focus on the specific needs of children in the different age groups. These three phases are:

Phase I: Emphasizes a wide range of movement patterns for primary school age children.

Phase II: Focuses on the athletic form with children concentrating on personal achievement rather than competition with other children. This is for upper elementary and middle school students.

Phase III: Is competitive and emphasizes skills, strategies, and techniques, as well as general good health for high school students.

Pertinent to the discussion here is the consideration of *Phase I* which was developed for children age 6–9. Some of these recommendations have been delineated by Stidwill[8] in the highlights that follow:

1. Children learn a wide range of movement characteristics to introduce them to different exercise patterns. Focus on fun, but work on and refine basic movement patterns. Use running activities—prediction runs and whistle runs—as part of the program.

2. After they run, encourage the children to perform easy, dynamic stretches. Use imagery, tell the children they are branches swaying in the wind. Static stretching, besides being boring, is of limited use to children in this phase since they are unlikely to generate enough force to injure themselves.

3. Keep mechanics simple. For instance, in the sprint use a standing start rather than the bunch start, and have the children run on the lines separating the lanes so that they will run in straight lines. These children should perform the shotput from a power position. Make sure the children understand the motions. Describe the activities using cue words like "shotpush" to describe the motion of the shotput, or tell them to imagine they are throwing a pie into the face of

---

[7]Werner, P. and Almond, L. Rethinking Track and Field as Sport in Public Schools, *Journal of Physical Education, Recreation, and Dance,* 60, 1989.

[8]Stidwill, Howard, Track and Field for All Ages, *Strategies,* January 1993.

someone taller—a coach, an older brother or sister—so they will know the correct angle of release for the shotput. (Incidentally, Davis and Isaacs[9] report that elementary school age children can generally handle shots weighing between four and eight pounds; the regulation weight for the college shot is 16 pounds, for high school, 12 pounds, and for junior high, 8 pounds.)

4. Modify the equipment for these young athletes, as in the case of the shotput above. For the high jump use ropes tied together and have children loosely hold each end. This offers children greater opportunities to participate and minimizes their fears about hitting the crossbar. When the children jump off constructed boxes, "touch the sky," and land in the sand, they become familiar with the basic conditioning exercises and skill components of the long jump. Make sure that modified equipment does not foster poor techniques. For instance, a softball may be an effective substitute for a shotput, but a child may end up throwing it with too much wrist action.

5. When it comes time to compete, do not put the children only in their strong events. Place them in a variety of running, jumping, and throwing events. Specialization comes later. (It may be interesting for the reader to know that this three-phase framework is used by the previously-mentioned Junior Olympic Program.)

Distance Running for Children

Just a few short years ago distance running for children was held in great disrepute, just as marathon running was for women. However, the last 12 to 15 years have seen a great change in attitude about distance running for children. The major reason for this appears to focus around the belief by some that health practices begun in early childhood are related to adult health and fitness. What we are essentially concerned with here is *aerobic* fitness provided by distance running. Charles O. Dotson,[10] my distinguished associate and coeditor of the research annual, *Exercise Physiology: Current Selected Research,* has asserted that there is evidence that certain health and fitness characteristics track from childhood into adulthood. Aerobic fitness is one of these characteristics. For

---

[9]Davis, Robert G. and Isaacs, Larry D., *Elementary Physical Education,* Winston-Salem, NC, 1992.

[10]Dotson, C., Criterion Reference Standard: Aerobic Fitness, *Journal of Physical Education, Recreation and Dance,* September, 1988.

example, a child who has above average aerobic fitness can be expected to track to middle age at above average aerobic fitness, while a child with below average aerobic fitness can be expected to track to middle age at below average aerobic fitness.

It is believed that one needs to have 42 millimeters of oxygen per kilogram of body weight per minute (42 ml/kg/min) to provide resistance against cardiovascular disease. In order to track to a level that is above 42 it is recommended that one participate in aerobic activity three times per week for 20 to 30 minutes periods.

Children should be provided with knowledge and motivation to develop habitual physical activity over and above that provided in regular school physical education classes. Thus, children should have the opportunity to participate in out-of-school aerobic activities. It is interesting to note that children who participate with parents who are fit are more likely to be fit than children who do not do so. Moreover, the more that community programs provide opportunities for physical activity in the form of aerobics for children, the more such children are likely to be aerobically fit.

It is interesting to note that test batteries developed for fitness of children now include a measure of aerobic fitness, usually in the form of a distance run/walk item. Among the organizations that provide for tests of fitness for children are the American Alliance for Health, Physical Education, Recreation, and Dance (Physical Best) and the Institute for Aerobic Research (Fitnessgram). Although the majority of fitness assessment batteries now include grades kindergarten through four, there is not a great deal of scientific evidence to substantiate the practicality, reliability, or validity of the various test items for children at these early age levels. In this general regard, Rikli, Petray, and Baumgartner[11] conducted a study of the reliability of distance run tests for children in grades K–4. The purpose of this study was to determine test-retest reliability for the 1-mile, 3/4-mile, and 1/2-mile distance run/walk tests for children in grades K–4. Fifty-one intact physical education classes were randomly assigned to one of the three distance run conditions. A total of 1,229 (621 boys, 608 girls) completed the test-retests in the fall (October), with 1,050 of these students (543 boys, 507 girls) repeating the tests in the spring (May).

The researchers concluded that results of this study indicate that the distance run can be utilized as a reliable assessment tool for students in

---

[11]Rikli, Roberta E., Petray, Clayre, and Baumgartner, Ted A., The Reliability of Distance Run Tests for Children in Grades K–4., *Research Quarterly for Exercise and Sport,* September 1992.

grade K–4 when appropriate age/distance adjustments are made. The 1-mile run/walk has acceptable norm-referenced reliability for students in Grades 3 and 4, with the ½ mile the longest acceptable distance for students in grades K and 1. For students in grade 2, the ½ and ¾ mile tests tend to be the most reliable with respect to overall estimates across both males and females in the fall. By the end of the school year (May), the ¾ and 1-mile tests tend to have the best overall reliabilities for 2nd graders. It might be argued that the ¾-mile run-walk should be the recommended distance for grade 2 students, both with respect to test reliability and as a logical transition between the ½-mile distance in grades K and 1 and the 1-mile test in grades 3 and 4.

Results of the study also indicate that test scores for most age/gender groups, with some exceptions for ages 5 and 6 on the 1-mile test, are acceptably reliable in their classification of students with respect to meeting the standards of the Physical Best and Fitnessgram national test batteries.

GYMNASTICS

The term *gymnastics* got its name from the building called the *gymnasium*, used in ancient Greece for purposes of training for the Olympic Games. The literal meaning of the Greek term gymasium means "naked art" because originally gymnastic exercises were performed in the nude.

Modern gymnastics were started in Germany in the early 19th century. This interest spread to England and finally to the United States.

In our country, interest of children in gymnastics probably had its start in the late 19th century. In 1889, there occurred an interesting episode at a "Conference in the Interest of Physical Training" in the city of Boston. At that time school administrators were beginning to feel the pressure and need for some kind of formal physical activity as a genuine part of the school program. Acting in a conservative manner at the conference, the school administrators proposed that a "physical training" program might be introduced as a part of the school day but that it must take little time, cost little money, and take place in the classroom. The Swedish System of Gymnastics was proposed as an exercise program for the classroom and on June 24, 1890, the Boston School Committee voted that this system of gymnastics be introduced in all of the public schools of Boston. Since this modest beginning, some form of gymnastics have

been an important part of most well-balanced physical education programs of our modern elementary schools.

In the school situation we often think of the broad area of *self-testing
activities*. These activities are the type that involve competing against
one's self and natural forces rather than with an opponent. These activities are based upon the child's desire to test his ability in such a way that
he attempts to better his or her own performance. This is a broad term
and involves such activities as stunts and tumbling, exercises with or
without appartus, and individual proficiency such as throwing for accuracy and/or distance and jumping for height and distance.

In recent years some individuals have resurrected the term "educational
gymnastics" to describe these kinds of activities. This term was used
around the turn of the century and was in contrast to the term "medical
gymnastics," which was used to identify activities used to correct a
certain functional or organic disability or deformity.

With regard to the so-called educational gymnastics the following
comments by Davis and Isaacs[12] are of interest.

> Another approach begun in the '70s was educational gymnastics, which allows
> children to explore movement on apparatus. In educational gymnastics, benches,
> poles, boxes, and other equipment (often interconnected) are used to explore
> ways to balance, vault or travel. An exploratory teaching approach using
> questions or problems to solve through movement is used . . . Unlike gymnastics,
> there are no spotters or explanation/demonstrations . . . It is the similarity
> between formal and educational gymnastic performance and equipment where
> legal problems arise. Well-meaning teachers unwittingly put themselves into
> liability situations by practicing educational gymnastics without setting appro-
> priate safety guidelines. In court cases involving injuries, teachers who prac-
> tice educational gymnastics have been successfully sued. The formal approach,
> however, has specific rules and guidelines which can be taught, and the
> teacher, through knowledge, can protect himself/herself. The open-ended
> educational gymnastics approach, however, is more difficult to teach and can
> be harder to defend legally.

Recently, I examined a large number of elementary school physical
education textbooks and found that about 90 percent use the term "self-
testing activities" while only about 10 percent use the term "educational
gymnastics."

At the primary level children should be given the opportunity to
participate in self-testing activities that are commensurate with their

---

[12]Davis, Robert G. and Isaacs, Larry D., *Elementary Physical Education,* Winston-Salem, NC, 1992.

ability. For example, stunts which involve imitations of animals are of great interest to boys and girls at this age level. Tumbling activities which involve some of the simple rolls are also suitable. Simple apparatus activities involving the use of equipment as horizontal ladders, low parallel and horizontal bars, balance beams, and climbing ropes can be utilized.

Self-testing activities at the intermediate level should be somewhat more advanced provided the children have had previous experience and teaching in this type of activity at the primary level. Tumbling activities that involve more advanced rolls and various kinds of body springs may be successfully introduced. Children at the intermediate level may continue to take part in apparatus using much the same equipment that was used at the primary level but moving to more advanced skills. When properly taught, apparatus activities are greatly enjoyed and are excellent for muscular development, especially for the torso and arms.

Gymnastics that are engaged in in out-of-school settings are more of a competitive nature and tend to attract those more highly skilled children. As mentioned in Chapter 1, these children are likely to start at an early age. Recent interest in gymnastics among children has been generated largely by recent successes of Americans, particularly girls, in the Olympic Games and national and world championships. These events have attracted large television audiences, not only among adults, but children as well.

GOLF

Although it is difficult to determine the exact time when the game of golf originated, it is believed that the place of its origin was Scotland. There is some evidence that golf was played in America in the 17th century; however, it was not until 1888 that the first permanent golf club, the St. Andrews Golf Club of Yonkers, New York was organized.[13]

We cannot say precisely when golf ceased to be a "rich man's" game and became a game for the "common man." It is possible that this might have occurred in the 1930s during the Great Depression. This activity soon became a family affair and this could mark the time of the beginning of children's interest in the game of golf.

---

[13]*The New Columbia Encyclopedia,* New York, Columbia Press, Edited by William H. Harris and Judith S. Levy, 1975.

Over the years there have been various golf programs for children. One of the more recent and highly successful ones is the *Hook a Kid on Golf.* This is a three-level program piloted at Emerald Dunes Golf Course in West Palm Beach, Florida in 1990. By 1992, 70 programs were held in 26 states introducing over 1300 new members to the game of golf. Florida led the way with six programs held while Virginia and Ohio were close behind with five sites each.

Through its three-level program, Hook a Kid on Golf gives children, who normally would not have the opportunity, the chance to learn and play the sport of golf. The mission is to give children, who in the past have been limited to other sports, the same opportunities to play golf by eliminating obstacles such as cost of instruction, lack of parental knowledge and purchase of equipment. Hook a Kid on Golf is a national membership program being administered by the National Youth Sports Coaches Association (NYSCA). The program has the support of the United States Golf Association, PGA Tour, LPGA, the National Golf Foundation, and the PGA of America. The three levels are Tee Level, Green Level and Challenge Level.

The *Tee Level* of the program is a free, week-long clinic in which locally sponsored children receive instruction, a starter set of golf clubs and other golf supplies. The clinic covers all aspects of the game including swing fundamentals, chipping and putting and also special talks on rules and etiquette, golf course maintenance, and drug awareness. This level is highlighted by an end of the week golf outing in which sponsors have the opportunity to participate with children in their first on-course golf experience. Tee Level Clinics are run locally by a Site Coordinator who is responsible for conducting the program and also communicating with the national office about specific procedures of the program.

After completing the Tee Level the children advance to the *Green Level.* Through the cooperation of local golf facilities, Green Level members are able to continue to practice and learn the skills of the game. Members of the Green Level receive a bimonthly newsletter from the national office with practice tips and information about rules and etiquette. The Green Level culminates when members apply for and pass a USGA approved rules test and a skills test developed by PGA professionals.

After passing the above tests, children reach the *Challenge Level.* In this final level of the program, members are challenged to play ten rounds of golf in accordance with the USGA's Junior Par System and to obtain a USGA handicap. Members completing the Challenge Level receive a Hook a Kid on Golf Lifetime Member card.

The program was funded originally by the NTSCA with the USGA providing a matching funds grant to help expand the program nationwide. On the local level, $100.00 sponsorships are solicited by the Site Coordinator for each child to participate in the three-level program. This includes one week of instruction whereby each child participating receives and keeps a starter set of Northwestern golf clubs with a bag, Spalding Top-Flite golf ball and visor, a Hook a Kid on Golf shirt, and membership into the three-level program. Each child also receives a member's bag tag for each level of the program and the bimonthly newsletter, *Tee to Green.*

In closing this final chapter, I will come full circle by repeating a theme made at the outset. I have tried to provide information that I hope will serve as a sensible guide for those adults—coaches, parents, and others—who are involved or plan to become involved in children's sports in a way that will always be in the best interest of the child, physically, socially, emotionally, and intellectually.

BIBLIOGRAPHY

American Academy of Pediatrics, *Physical Fitness and the Schools*, 80, 1987.

American College of Sports Medicine, Opinion Statement of Physical Fitness in Children and Youth, *Medicine and Science in Sport and Exercise*, 4, 1988.

Backx, F. J. G., et al, Sports Injuries in School-Age Children, *American Journal of Sports Medicine*, April, 1989.

Baranowski, T., et al, Aerobic Physical Activity Among Third and Sixth Grade Elementary School Children, *Journal of Developmental and Behavioral Pediatrics*, 8, 1987.

Baranowski, T., et al, Reliability and Validity of Children's Self-Report of Aerobic Activity, *Research Quarterly for Exercise and Sports*, 55, 1984.

Bar-Or, O., A Commentary to Children and Fitness: A Public Health Perspective, *Research Quarterly for Exercise and Sports*, 58, 1987.

Bar-Or, O., *Pediatric Sports Medicine for the Practitioner: From Physiological Principles to Clinical Applications*, New York, Springer-Verlag, 1983.

Bar-Or, O., *Pediatric Sports Medicine*, M. Katz and E. R. Stehin Eds., New York, Springer-Verlag, 1983.

Blais, M. R. and Vallerand, R. J., Multimodal Effects of Electromyographic Biofeedback: Looking at Children's Ability to Control Precompetition Anxiety, *Journal of Sports Psychology*, December 1986.

Blimke, C. J. R., Strength Training for the Child Athlete, *Scholastic Coach*, October 1989.

Bredemeier, B. J., et al, The Relationship of Sport Involvement with Children's Moral Reasoning and Aggressive Tendencies, *Journal of Sports Psychology*, December 1986.

Brustad, R. J., Affective Outcomes in Competitive Youth Sports: The Influence of Interpersonal and Socialization Factors, *Journal of Sport and Exercise Psychology*, September 1988.

Brustad, R. J. and Weiss, M., Competence Perception and Sources of Worry in High, Medium and Low Competitive Trait-Anxious Young Athletes, *Journal of Sports Psychology*, June 1987.

Coakley, J., A Sociological Perspective, In M. Weiss and D. Gould, Eds., *Sport for Children and Youth*, Champaign, IL, Human Kinetics, 1986.

Cureton, K. J., Distance Running Performance Tests in Children: What do They Mean?, *Journal of Physical Education, Recreation and Dance*, 53, 1982.

197

Debu, B., Woollacott, M. and Mowatt, M., Development of Postural Control in Children: Effects of Gymnastics Training, In Clarke, J. E. and Humphrey, J. H., Eds., *Advances in Motor Development Research,* New York, AMS Press, 1987.

Dixon, R., Playing the Game (moves designed to stop children from overdoing it) *The Times Educational Supplement,* January 1988.

Duda, J. L., Toward a Developmental Theory of Children's Motivation in Sport, *Journal of Sports Psychology,* June 1987.

Epstein, L. H., et al, Long-Term Relationship Between Weight and Aerobic-Fitness Change in Children, *Health Psychology,* 7, 1988.

Fischman, M. G. and Schneider, T., Skill Level, Vision, and Proprioception in Simple One-Hand Catching, *Journal of Motor Behavior,* 17, 1989.

Freedson, P. S., et al, Energy Expenditure in Prepubescent Children: Influences of Sex and Age, *American Journal of Clinical Nutrition,* 34, 1981.

Friedlander, Royce B. and Lohmeyer, Roxanne, E., A Place to Start: Games and Sports Tasks for Young Children, *Journal of Physical Education, Recreation and Dance,* September 1988.

Goldberg, Barry, Children, Sports, and Chronic Disease, *Physician and Sports Medicine,* October 1990.

Grupe, O., Top-Level Sports for Children from an Educational Viewpoint, *International Journal of Physical Education,* 22, 1985.

Hopper, C., *The Sports Confident Child,* New York, Pantheon Books, 1988.

Krahenbuhl, G. S., Morgan, D. W., and Pangrazi, R. P., Longitudinal Changes in Distance-Running Performance of Young Males, *International Journal of Sports Medicine,* 10, 1989.

Krahenbuhl, G. S., Skinner, J. S., and Kohrt, W. M., Developmental Aspects of Maximal Aerobic Power in Children, In R. L. Terjung, Ed., *Exercise and Sport Science Reviews,* 13, 1985.

Langendorfer, Stephen, et al, Children's Acquatics: Managing the Risk, *Parks and Recreation,* February 1989.

Malina, R. M., Competitive Youth Sports and Biological Maturation, In E. W. Brown and C. F. Branta, Eds, *Competitive Sports for Children and Youth: An Overview of Research and Issues,* Champaign, IL, Human Kinetics, 1988.

Mazenco, C. and Gross, J. B., A Comparative Study of the Traditional Children's Game of Softball vs. the Modified Rules of T–Ball, *New Zealand Journal of Health, Physical Education and Recreation,* 24, 1991.

McConnell, A. and Wade, G., Effects of Lateral Ball Location, Grade, and Sex in Catching, *Perceptual and Motor Skills,* 70, 1990.

Micheli, L. J., Making Youth Sports Safe and Enjoyable, *Scholastic Coach,* April 1988.

Micheli, L. J., Prevent Children's Sports Injuries, *PTA Today,* March 1983.

Noland, Melody, et al, The Measurement of Physical Activity in Young Children, *Research Quarterly for Exercise and Sports,* 61, 1990.

Pelham, William E., Jr., et al, Methylphenidate and Baseball Playing in ADHD Children: Who's On First?, *Journal of Consulting and Clinical Psychology,* February 1990.

Podolsky, M. Lawrence, Don't Rule Out Sports for Hypertensive Children, *Physical and Sports Medicine,* September 1989.

Remak, Bruce, Starting Them Right, Helping Parents Prepare Young Children for Sports, *Strategies,* September–October 1988.

Roberton, M. A., Changing Motor Patterns During Childhood, In J. R. Thomas Ed., *Motor Development During Childhood and Adolescence,* Minneapolis, Burgess, 1984.

Rotella, Robert and Bunker, Linda K., Parenting Your Superstar, How to Help Your Child Get the Most Out of Sports, Champaign, IL, Human Kinetics, 1987.

Rowland, T. W., Aerobic Response to Endurance Training in Prepubescent Children: A Critical Analysis, *Medicine and Science in Sports and Exercise,* 17, 1985.

Smyth, M. M., and Marriott, A. M., Vision and Proprioception in Simple Catching, *Journal of Motor Behavior,* 14, 1982.

Strohmeyer, H. S., Williams, K., and Schaub-George, D., Developmental Sequences for Catching a Small Ball: A Prelongitudinal Screening, *Research Quarterly for Exercise and Sports,* 62, 1991.

Tacha, Karolyn K., et al, Sports Fitness School for Children, *Journal of Physical Education, Recreation and Dance,* September 1984.

Taft, T. N., Sports Injuries in Children, *Elementary School Journal,* May 1991.

Thorland, W. and Gilliam, T., Comparison of Serum Lipids Between Habitually High and Low Active Pre-Adolescent Males, *Medicine and Science in Sports and Exercise,* 13, 1981.

Wankel, M. and Sefton, J. M., A Season-Long Investigation of Fun in Youth Sports, *Journal of Sport and Exercise Psychology,* December 1989.

Weiss, Maureen R. and Horn, Thelma S., The Relation Between Children's Accuracy Estimates of Their Physical Competence and Achievement Related Characteristics, *Research Quarterly for Exercise and Sports,* 61, 1990.

Weiss, Maureen R., Youth Sports: Is Winning Everything? *Childhood Education,* Summer 1989.

Williams, M. H. Weight Control Through Exercise and Diet for Children and Young Athletes, *Academy Papers: American Academy of Physical Education,* Champaign, IL 1985.

INDEX

A

Agility, 43
Anger, 68
Angle recession, 11
Auditory perception, 97–98
Auxiliary skills, 107–109
Axial, skills, 106

B

Balance, 43
Baseball, 155–164
Baseball skills, 156–160
   baserunning, 159–160
   batting, 158–159
   fielding, 157–158
   games to practice, 163–164
   pitching, 158
   throwing
Basic sports skills for children, 99–118
Basketball, 166–176
Basketball skills, 167–174
   catching, 169–170
   dribbling, 172
   games to practice, 175–176
   guarding, 173
   passing, 168–169
   pivoting, 173
   rebounding, 173–174
   shooting, 170–172
Blood pressure, 77
Blood sugar analysis, 77
Body awareness, 89–90

C

Catching, 115–117

Characteristics of childhood emotionality, 66–67
Characteristics of good teachers, 120–121
Child development and sports, 19–33
Childrens' attitudes toward coaches, 16–17
Chorioretinal rupture, 11
Circulatory-respiratory endurance, 43
Coach or parent as teacher of sports, 118–134
Coaches' Code of Ethics, 13–14
Competition as a factor in children's sports, 7–10
Coordination, 43

D

Development of skill and ability, 29–30
Diaphysis, 12
Directionality of sound, 130–131
Distance running for children, 189–191
Dodging, 108

E

Emotional arousals and reactions, 67–69
Emotional aspect of personality, 25–26
Emotional control, 33
Emotional development of children through sports, 65–80
   guidelines for, 72–74
Emotional needs of children, 69–71
Emotional objectives of sports, 31–32
Epiphyses, 12
Evaluating contributions of sports to emotional development, 77–80
Evaluating contributions of sports to social development, 61–64

F

Factors concerning emotional development, 65–69
Factors involved in learning skills, 100–101
Falling, 109
Fear, 67
Flag football, 145–146
Flexibility
Football, 135–146
Football skills, 138–143
    blocking and tackling, 143
    carrying the ball, 141
    catching, 140–141
    centering the ball, 141–142
    games to practice, 143–145
    passing, 139–140
    place kicking, 142
    punting, 142
Fun and emotional release, 32–33

G

Galloping, 105
Galvanic skin response, 77
Games to practice baseball skills, 163–164
Games to practice basketball skills, 175–176
Games to practice football skills, 143–145
Games to practice soccer skills, 152–154
Games to practice volleyball skills, 182–184
Golf, 193–195
Gymnastics, 191–193

H

Historical background of children's sports, 4–7
Hopping, 104–105
How children feel when they lose, 31–32
How children feel when they win, 31
Human demonstration, 131–132
Hyphemia, 11

I

Improving perceptual-motor development through sports, 87
Individual sports, 185–195

Injuries as a factor in children's sports, 10–12
Intellectual aspect of personality, 26–27
Intellectual development of children through sports, 81–97
    guidelines for, 85–86
Intellectual needs of children, 81–85
Intellectual objectives of children's sports, 34

J

Jealousy, 68–69
Joy, 69
Jumping, 104

K

Kicking, 115–115
Kinesthesis, 92
Kinesthetic perception, 92–93

L

Landing, 109
Laterality and directionality, 90–91
Leaping, 103–104
Learning products of sports, 124
Locomotor skills, 101–106

M

Maintaining a suitable level of physical fitness, 28–29
Maturity, 65
Meaning of child development, 20–23
Meaning of learning, 122
Meaning of teaching, 122
Mini-volleyball, 177
Muscular endurance, 42–43
Muscular power, 43
Muscular strength, 42

O

Objectives of sports for children, 27–34
One Old Cat, 155
Ossification, 12

Osteochondritis capitulum, 11
Overarm throwing pattern, 112–113

P

Parents' Code of Ethics, 14
Perceptual-motor skills, 87–89
Phases of the teaching-learning situation,
    128–134
    auditory input, 128–131
    evaluation, 133–134
    participation, 132–133
    visual input, 131–132
Physical aspect of personality, 23–24
Physical activity yield, 45–48
Physical development of children through
    sports, 35–38
    guidelines for, 39–41
Physical needs of children, 35–39
Physical objectives of sports for children,
    27–30
Pivoting, 108
Pulse rate, 77
President's Council on Physical Fitness, 5

R

Research in emotional behavior of children,
    75–77
Research in social behavior of children, 58–61
Retinal edema, 11
Running, 102–103

S

Secondary glaucoma, 11
Sidearm throwing pattern, 111–112
Skill level, 99
Skills as specific sports events, 117–118
Skills of propulsion and retrieval, 109–115
Skipping, 105–106
Sliding, 106
Soccer, 146–154
Soccer skills, 147–152
    body traps, 149–150
    dribbling, 148
    foot traps, 150
    games to practice, 152–154

    kicking, 147–148
    heading, 148–149
    leg traps, 150–151
    tackling, 151–152
    throw in, 149
Social aspect of personality, 24–25
Social development of children through
    sports, 49–64
    guidelines for, 54–57
Social distance scales, 62–63
Social needs of children, 51–54
Social objectives of sports for children, 30
Sociograms, 62
Sociographs, 62
Softball, 164–165
Some principles of learning applied to sports,
    124–128
Speed, 43
Sports errors, 99
Sportsmanship, 63–64
Starting, 107
Stopping, 107–108
Striking, 113–114
Supervision of childrens' sports, 12–18
Swimming, 185–187

T

Tactile perception, 94
Teaching and learning in sports, 121–124
Throwing, 119–113
Total development of the child, 19–25
Touch football, 145–146
Track and field, 187–191

U

Underarm throwing pattern, 110–111

V

Volleyball, 176–184
Volleyball skills, 177–181
    games to practice, 182–184
    net recovery, 181
    serving, 179–180
    the block, 181
    the set, 180

Volleyball skills (*Continued*)
   the spike, 180–181
   volleying, 177–179
     Visual perception, 94–97
Visual symbols, 131

W

Walking, 102
Worry, 67–68